ETHICS IN EARLY BUDDHISM

ETHICS IN EARLY BUDDHISM

David J. Kalupahana

HAWAI'I

University of Hawai'i Press, Honolulu

Printed in the United States of America

95 96 97 98 99 00 5 4 3 2 1

Library of Congress Cataloging-in-Publication Data

Kalupahana, David J., 1933–
Ethics in early Buddhism / David J. Kalupahana.
p. cm.
Includes bibliographical references and index.
ISBN 0–8248–1702–8 (Alk. paper)
1. Buddhist ethics. 2. Buddhism—Doctrines—History—Early period, to ca. 250 B.C. I. Title
BJ1289.K35 1995
294.3'5—dc20 94–43468
CIP

University of Hawai'i Press books are printed on acid-free paper and meet the guidelines for permanence and durability of the Council on Library Resources

Book design by Kenneth Miyamoto

CONTENTS

PREFACE vii
ABBREVIATIONS ix

PART ONE
HISTORICAL BACKGROUND AND PROBLEMS

1 Pre-Buddhist Indian Moral Theories and Their Ultimate Developments 3
2 Knowledge 26
3 The Fact-Value Distinction 37
4 The World and the Will 47
5 Individual and Society 54

PART TWO
THE MORAL LIFE, THE PRINCIPLE, AND JUSTIFICATION

6 The Noble Life *(Brahmacariya)* 65
7 Virtues: The Beginning of the Way 70
8 The Eightfold Path: The Middle of the Way 77
9 Freedom: The Conclusion of the Way 84
10 The Status of the Moral Principle 90
11 Justification of the Moral Life 96

PART THREE
APPLICATIONS OF THE PRINCIPLE

12 Society and Morals 113
13 Economics and Morals 119
14 Politics and Morals 124

15 Law, Justice, and Morals 130
16 Nature and Morals 137
17 Conclusion: The Stream and the Lotus Pond 143

NOTES 147
GLOSSARY 159
SELECT BIBLIOGRAPHY 163
INDEX 167

PREFACE

THE PRESENT volume is devoted to an analysis of the materials available primarily in the early discourses *(sutta)* and to some extent in the books on discipline *(vinaya).* Part one is devoted to a survey of the pre-Buddhist background as well as some of the problems relating to ethical theory. While the general understanding was that in this background the major moral theory was deontology, which culminated in the *Bhagavadgītā,* I have indicated that a strong utilitarian trend of thought was also present and that it was this utilitarianism that was utilized by Kauṭilya in his *Arthaśāstra.* Since the *Bhagavadgītā* and the *Arthaśāstra* were finalized during the same period (circa 400 B.C.), and since these two moral philosophies would have continued side by side with the moral philosophy presented by the Buddha, it was thought that tracing their development until the two traditions assumed final form would provide a better view of the Buddhist theory as well.

This account of historical background is followed by an analysis of problems that have haunted philosophers since critical thinking first appeared. Prominent among these is the problem relating to knowledge, which then spreads into other areas such as the distinctions between facts and values, the individual will and the world will, individual and society, and so on. A clarification of these issues, especially as they appear in the context of early Buddhism was considered to be relevant to an understanding of the moral philosophy of early Buddhism.

Part two deals with the moral life as expounded in the discourses. In a small monograph like the present it would be impossible to treat all the moral concepts discussed in the innumerable discourses. The strategy adopted here is to divide the path to moral perfection into three parts—

the beginning, the middle, and the conclusion, a division adopted by the Buddha himself—and analyze only the most important aspects listed under each of the parts. This, it is hoped, will provide a holistic view of the moral philosophy connecting its root to the fruit, the separation of which has led to much misunderstanding regarding the nature and status of the moral life. Since there is sufficient evidence that the Buddha began his career with a search for what is good *(kusala)* and that the moral principle was formulated after his attainment of moral perfection, a separate chapter on the nature and status of the principle follows the discussion of the moral life. The final chapter in part two deals with the prominence given to human life and the Buddha's justification of the moral life.

Part three deals with some applications of the moral principle in explaining some aspects of human life, such as the social organization, economics, politics, law and nature, or the environment. These have been selected because of their contemporary relevance. The order in which these topics are introduced is not significant. What is important is the understanding of the perspective from which the Buddha looked at these different aspects of human life.

ABBREVIATIONS

(All references to Pali texts are from the editions of the Pali Text Society, London.)

A	*Aṅguttara-nikāya*
D	*Dīgha-nikāya*
Dh	*Dhammapada*
HBP	*A History of Buddhist Philosophy*
It	*Itivuttaka*
M	*Majjhima-nikāya*
Pv	*Petavatthu*
S	*Saṃyutta-nikāya*
Sn	*Sutta-nipāta*
Thag	*Theragāthā*
Thig	*Therīgāthā*
Ud	*Udāna*
Vin	*Vinaya Piṭaka*

PART ONE

HISTORICAL BACKGROUND AND PROBLEMS

CHAPTER 1

Pre-Buddhist Indian Moral Theories and Their Ultimate Developments

INTELLIGENT human beings cannot resist the manner in which they come to be impressed by the nomological character of the physical world with its strong objective pull. In contrast, they experience difficulty in accounting for certain feelings and aspirations, especially those relating to freedom, the latter being the foundation of moral philosophy. In the view of even some of the more sophisticated philosophers, freedom therefore turns out to be an anomalous phenomenon. This is true not only in the context of modern physics and astronomy, but also in the world of the ancients, who observed the regularity with which natural phenomena function compared to their decisions about right and wrong, good and bad. While this experience has been the source of the sharp dichotomy between statements of facts on the one hand and discourses on values on the other, it also led to pervasive attempts to formulate moral laws equal to or even more absolute than the laws of physics and astronomy. The deontological systems in their undiluted and pure forms represent such endeavors.

Deontological System

In the ancient Indian context the search for a universal moral principle that could serve as a foundation for a harmonious community life was conducted within a framework that recognized a distinction between the celestial and the terrestrial. The gods of the Vedic pantheon were divided into these two spheres. Those like Indra, Varuṇa, Soma, Rudra, Parjanya, Yama, Mṛtyu, and Īśāna were regarded as celestial gods. They were individual gods worshipped at different times or occasions depending upon the needs and aspirations of the worshipper. Thus, even though there was a plurality of gods, at the time the favor of any one of the gods was invoked, that particular god was looked upon as the one unitary god. The terrestrial gods, some of whom were already enjoying celestial status, were mentioned in numbers or groups as Vaśus, Rudras, Ādityas, Viśvedevas, and Maruts. The earth itself was represented by a singular god, Puṣan, who is feminine.

The first important conception of a moral order emerged in the background of this division of the universe into celestial and terrestrial spheres. This concept was referred to as *ṛta.* The initial inspiration for the formulation of the conception of *ṛta* was the observed physical order or the uniformity of nature.[1] *Ṛta* as the moral order was not created but found a guardian and an enforcer in Varuṇa, who, therefore, turned out to be the moral god of the Vedic pantheon. What Varuṇa had in his custody, namely the moral order, like its physical counterpart, was a celestial phenomenon and a power external to human beings. Speculation was already rampant as to whether these gods were one or many,[2] with the Vedic thinkers favoring the conception of one or unity, primarily because the celestial had to be the context in which unity, if there were to be any idea of unity, could be located. During the time when Varuṇa held sway as the guardian of the *ṛta,* the other gods were relegated to the background. Thus, *ṛta,* as both the natural and the moral orders and being celestial, was binding on all earthlings. The obligation to follow it is therefore derived from its celestial status.

It seems that as speculation progressed leading into the period represented by the *Upaniṣads,* especially the pre-Buddhistic ones, the *Bṛhadāraṇyaka* and the *Chāndogya,* the moral order appeared to be totally extraneous—so much so that a human being would wonder whether he or she had any capacity at all even to emulate that order. The existence of an inviolable celestial order does not necessarily mean that a human being—a terrestrial creature—also has the capacity to follow that order. In the absence of the latter, the former would be rendered useless as a way of restraining the human behavior for which it is intended. It is very possible that this is the reason for the conception of *ṛta* to sink into oblivion and to be replaced by the notions of *ātma* and *brahma.*

It is true that *ātma* and *brahma* are generally understood to be interchangeable terms. They came to be used as such after the recognition that ultimate freedom is achieved through the realization of oneness or identity of the two. The subtle difference between the two can be observed when we examine one of the early references in the *Bṛhadāraṇyaka*.[3] *Ātma* is used here specifically to refer to the ultimate reality within the human and the outside world, while the term *brahma* is employed to express the ultimate value from which is derived the four social classes and their duties *(dharma)*.

Whatever the religious justification of *ātma* may have been at any point in the evolution of the concept, the philosophical need for it was paramount. As mentioned earlier, an objective moral law requires the capacity on the part of the human to abide by that law. The ordinary empirical human with his or her impermanent physical personality as well as a fluctuating, unsteady, and fickle psychic personality does not have the strength and stability to withstand the demands of the moral law. Hence, there is the need for a real self in the human that can stand apart from the unstable psychophysical personality and that can serve as an "inner controller" *(antaryāmin)*[4] guiding the human toward the realization of *brahma*, the ultimate moral Absolute. The two selves are graphically illustrated by the metaphor of two birds perched on the same branch, one enjoying the sweet *pipplava* fruit, that is, the pleasures of sense, undistracted by higher moral concerns (the egoistic empirical self), while the other maintains an eternal vigilance, unblinking, in order to guarantee that the moral law is not violated (the transcendental self).[5] Once the conception of the real self is philosophically justified and established, the next step is to relate and align it with the moral absolute.

The significance of the *Bṛhadāraṇyaka* passage where the social institution of caste is derived from *brahma* cannot be ignored.[6] If the concept of *ātma* represents the ultimately real self, it has actually very little to do with morality itself, except accommodating the capacity on the part of the human to be moral. Morality involves more than oneself; otherwise there will be only "moral solitude." It relates to one's behavior in the context of a society of individuals. The moral law represented by *brahma* is therefore invariably associated with the social order. However, in the Indian context, that social order pivoted for centuries around the fourfold caste system. According to the earlier sociological speculations, the four castes appeared as a result of the sacrifice of a mythical person *(puruṣa)* by the gods, his mouth being identified with the priestly caste *(brāhmaṇa)*, the arms with the warrior, or ruling, caste *(kṣatriya)*, the thighs with the productive segments of society such as farmers, merchants, and artisans *(vaiśya)*, while the servants *(śūdra)* were born from the feet.[7] The priestly caste was the custodian of the sacred literature, the *Vedas*, and hence officiated at the religious ceremonies. As such this caste was the intermediary between gods and humans, the celestial and the terrestrial. However, by the time of the *Upaniṣads*, the warrior, or ruling, caste was competing with the priestly caste for political power and domination and were actively engaged in an enterprise that previously was the exclusive vocation of the brahmans, namely, intellectual activity represented by philosophical speculation. Hence the *Bṛhadāraṇyaka* passage refers to the warrior class as the superior creation of *brahma.*

It is significant to note that *brahma* did not create the priestly, or *brāhmaṇa*, caste. The implication is that *brahma* is identical with *brāhmaṇa*, and hence the idea that anyone injuring a member of the *brāhmaṇa* caste attacks his own source. Subsequent to the creation of the warrior, or *kṣatriya*, caste, *brahma* created the other two castes, the *vaiśya* and the *śūdra.*

Although the conception of duty does not appear in the *Upaniṣads* in the elaborate form in which it came to be presented in the *Bhagavadgītā*, the seeds of this latter theory are indeed found in the former. The creation of *dharma* subsequent to the creation of the three castes would mean that the *dharma* is to be derived from what preceded, namely, the coming into existence of all four castes. It is therefore possible to interpret *dharma* in this particular context, not as the moral law identical with *brahma*, but as *svadharma*, which involves the more restricted sense of duty assigned to each caste as in the *Bhagavadgītā.*

At this point in the evolution of Indian thought, *brahma* acquires more power than that assigned to physical forces, whereas in the conception of *ṛta* the moral and natural orders occupied equal status and were complementary. The *Kena Upaniṣad* contains the legend of *brahma* appearing before the gods. Gods did not know who or what *brahma* was. They deputed Agni, the god of fire, to ascertain its identity. He, boasting of his power to burn, was challenged by *brahma* to burn a straw, but was baffled. Unsuccessful, Agni returned to the gods, and Vāyu, the god of wind, was sent on the mission. He, vaunting his power to blow anything away, was likewise challenged to blow a straw away and was likewise baffled.[8]

Bṛhadāraṇyaka, in its famous dialogue between Yajñavalkya and Gārgī, presents *brahma* as the foundation on which all other worlds rest.[9]

The admission that the gods are not pleased that humans should know this ultimate truth—for then they would know the subordinate place the gods hold and give up making offerings[10]—seems to be a metaphorical way of expressing the idea that humans should be striving for the ideal instead of attempting to comprehend it. This may go against the generally held view that *brahma* is to be known by transcending all ordinary forms of knowledge and developing what is regarded as a yogic intuition. Such a knowledge claim was to come subsequently, especially in the later *Upaniṣads,*[11] which still leaves open the question as to whether everyone who follows the path leading to *brahma* does so with understanding. The answer almost always is that unquestioned faith in the veracity of the moral principle is what enables a person to follow it, and that it is the yogin who has directly perceived or realized it. It may be an acceptable religious hypothesis but a weak philosophical thesis. The early Upaniṣadic assertion is philosophically more consistent in that it rejects the idea that the ultimate truth, the noumenal *brahma,* can be known by a human.

In fact, the criticisms of the Materialists, who denied the meaningfulness of moral discourse, and the Buddha, who attempted to confine the moral principle to the terrestrial, seem to be the reasons for the later *Upaniṣads* to assert the knowability of *brahma* through yogic intuition. This idea finds elaboration in the *Bhagavadgītā,* compiled a few centuries after the emergence of Buddhism. While it endeavored to establish the later Upaniṣadic thesis that ultimate truth can be known by humans through the development of yogic insight, it was achieved at the sacrifice of humanness, or humanity, in the practice of the path leading to *brahma.*

Arjuna, the hero of the *Bhagavadgītā,* was reluctant to engage in battle against his kith and kin, fearing that it would lead to unnecessary death and destruction, thereby paving the way for the disintegration of the family, social structure, and moral and religious values. He therefore started as a utilitarian unwilling to cause pain and suffering to human beings, not prepared to disrupt the social fabric but willing to lay down even his own life in order to guarantee "maximum happiness." The philosophy of the *Bhagavadgītā* is a gigantic effort to discredit that utilitarian philosophy and establish what has come to be the absolutely pure and perfect system of deontological ethics.

To eliminate the initial remorse in Arjuna's mind about the destruction of human life resulting from an armed conflict, the *Bhagavadgītā* presents two arguments, the rational and the empirical, supporting the idea that the destruction of the human psychophysical personality does not imply the annihilation of the ultimately real self, the *ātma.* The rational argument is identified with the method of Sāṅkhya, a rationalist school upholding the view that "nothing comes out of nothing," or that "being cannot be non-being." The indestructible *ātma* is like the eternal and immutable primordial substance *(prakṛti)* pervading every phenomenon.[12] The empirical argument is not one based on ordinary human experience, but the insight of the yogin.[13] The *Bhagavadgītā,* coming after the Buddha's detailed analysis of the psychology of yoga to show the nonavailability of a permanent and eternal *ātma* as an object of yogic experience, provides an equally detailed description of the process of yoga, claiming that in the highest stage, when all the sensory faculties are withdrawn, the yogin realizes the *ātma.*

This claim, however, would create problems for the *Bhagavadgītā,* especially in view of the need to encourage Arjuna to perform his own duty *(svadharma),* which is to fight in the battle instead of pursuing a duty that is assigned to the *brāhmaṇa* caste, namely engaging in religious discipline aimed at realizing the ultimate truth. Thus, even though four alternative forms of endeavor are recommended in the text, only two are actually assigned to Arjuna. The four alternatives are described thus:

> Fix your mind on Me alone. Cause your intelligence *(buddhi)* to enter into Me. Thus you will dwell in Me thenceforward. There is no doubt about this.
>
> O, Conqueror of Wealth, if you are not able to concentrate your thought on Me, then seek to attain Me through the yoga of practice *(abhyāsa).*
>
> If you are incapable even of practice, be intent on My work. Even performing actions for My sake, you will attain perfection.
>
> However, if you are unable even to do this, then resort to My power. Abandon all the fruits of action, act with self-restraint.[14]

First is the possibility of reaching the ultimate reality or cognizing it through the intellectual faculty, which is yoga of knowledge *(jñāna).* The second is the yoga of practice, which involves continuous involvement in religious discipline. The third is performing actions for the sake of the Divine. This implies self-exertion on the part of Arjuna. The last is in fact abandoning everything to the power of the Divine.

The *Bhagavadgītā* has made an enormous attempt to strengthen the idea expressed in the *Bṛhadāraṇyaka* passage outlining the creation of the three lower castes from *brahma.* While the Upaniṣadic passage simply states this, the *Bhagavadgītā* goes further to explain the reality of the four castes by relating them to the three natural qualities *(guṇa):* the bright or the bouyant *(sattva),* the mobile or the active *(rajas)* and the dark or the heavy *(tamas),* a doctrine borrowed from the Sāṅkhya school. The first is predominant in the constitution of the *brāhmaṇa,* the second dominates the makeup of the *kṣatriya,* and the third is part and parcel of the nature of the *vaiśya* and *śūdra.*[15] Thus, the duties assigned to the four castes are based upon the innate natural qualities of each one and do not represent those of an arbitrary social classification. A duty so allocated is sacred. "Better is the doing of one's own duty *(svadharma)* however imperfectly carried out, than the duty of another carried out perfectly. He who follows the duties ordained *(niyata)* by his own nature does not incur sin."[16] These duties, as in any other deontological system, had to be performed without regard for consequences.

Arjuna, who appears not to be impressed by these arguments, was finally convinced of Kṛṣṇa's discourse only after he was asked to abandon "all duties" *(sarvadharma)* and take refuge in the Divine alone.[17] The duties of the four castes are those allocated on the basis of their being born as humans. The abandoning of all duties would therefore imply the renunciation of human nature or character. In other words, the best form of action is not merely one performed without concern for consequences or fruits, but also one that goes beyond humanity. Self-sacrifice thus turns out to be the ideal action. In such ideal action, Arjuna perceived an opportunity to follow the highest moral ideal any mortal may be expected to follow.[18] Such self-sacrifice can be justified only on the argument that *brahma,* the moral ideal, completely transcends terrestrial life. Thus, renouncing not only the interests of the mundane life but humanity itself constitues the royal road to freedom.

Utilitarianism

While deontological thinking emerged as a result of the belief in absolute laws combined with the theory of social classes *(varṇa)* and came to dominate the entire cultural and religious life of the Indians after it received strongly religious and spiritual coloring in the *Bhagavadgītā,* there was another pervasive utilitarian trend of thought that has so far received scant attention from scholars interested in Indian philosophy. The religious and spiritual sanction that deontology received seems to have kept this utilitarian trend under a veil of darkness.

In the Indian context deontology and utilitarianism belonged to two different cultures. While the *Bhagavadgītā* represents the ultimate development of the deontology of the Brahmanical tradition, which can be traced back to the *Puruṣa-sūkta* of the *Ṛgveda,*[19] utilitarianism was part of the tradition that came to be identified as the ascetic, or *śramaṇa.* The brahmans, who were dissatisfied with deontology, may have joined ranks with the ascetics; hence, the reference to *samaṇa-brāhmaṇa* in the description of the ascetic tradition. It may be remembered that the ascetics were strangers to the *Vedas.* For this reason, utilitarianism could be looked upon as being originally non-Aryan. Yet, one may wonder how and why such a moral theory could be associated with the ascetic tradition, which is generally perceived as otherworldly or world denying. It is possible to surmise that asceticism turned out to be an ivy that concealed utilitarian thought, especially at a time when opposition to Brahmanism was on the rise. But during the early stages utilitarianism and asceticism seem to have been separate yet related ways of life. This is evident from the manner in which the foundation of utilitarianism, namely, the theory of the four "stages of life" *(āśramadharma),* evolved.

The initial references to the theory of the stages of life are in the early *Upaniṣads, Chāndogya* and *Bṛhadāraṇyaka,* two treatises that also represent the intermingling of Aryan and non-Aryan cultures. These refer only to three stages. Beside the life of a student *(brahmacārin)* and a householder *(gṛhastha),* men might give themselves to ascetic practices *(vānaprastha)* in their search for truth.[20] Yet there was no determination that these three stages were to be followed in strict succession. The ascetic stage may follow the life of the householder or it may not. The majority of the householders did not adapt the ascetic life. It is only in the later *Upaniṣads* that we find the addition of a fourth state involving absolute renunciation *(saṃnyāsin)* as well as the ordering of the four as successive stages.[21]

Unlike the theory of the four castes *(varṇadharma)*, where the status of an individual in society is determined by the caste into which he or she is born, the theory of the four stages of life emphasizes the different stages a person occupies from birth to death. The final formulation of the stages of life is as follows: First is the life of a student devoted to traditional learning, participating in religious worship and rituals, depending on others for a living, and having unlimited respect for the teacher. The second stage is that of a householder, who earns a livelihood by engaging in a profession; marries among his equals (that is, within his caste); offers gifts to gods, ancestors, guests, and servants; and survives on what remains after he has taken care of the above obligations. The third stage is the life of a forest recluse, who observes chastity; leads a rough life, such as sleeping on bare ground and wearing deerskin; performs religious rit-uals; worships gods and ancestors; and survives primarily on food procurable in the forest. The final stage is that of the ascetic, who renounces the world, applies himself to the restraint of the senses, abstains from any kind of worldly activity, is without possessions, and lives by begging.[22] It seems that the duties assigned here to a person at different stages of his or her life would not be compatible with the set of duties prescribed by the *varṇadharma*. For example, according to the latter, the last two stages cannot be the duties assigned to a *vaiśya* or a *śūdra*, even if we allow such duties to a *kṣatriya*, who was considered to be the superior creation of *brahma*.[23]

However, the *āśramadharma* is quite compatible with the four fruits of life, or *puruṣārthas*. The four fruits of life are wealth *(artha)*, enjoyment of wealth *(kāma)*, morality *(dharma)*, and freedom *(mokṣa)*. There is no one-to-one correspondence between the four stages of life and the four fruits of life. For example, all four fruits can be considered appropriate for the householder even though freedom may be a distant but not immediate concern for him or her. The first two are certainly not meant for the recluse and the ascetic.

With the accommodation of the non-Aryan culture by the mainline Brahmanical tradition, the conceptions of the stages of life and the fruits of life on the one hand, and the theory of caste on the other, may have developed side by side. The latter was emphasized by the Brahmanical tradition because it enabled the *brāhmaṇa* class to dominate the other three classes. The former were favored by those who were rejecting the Brahmanical claims. Even though the Buddha was a critic of the Brahmanical tradition and belonged to the so-called ascetic tradition, he was unwilling to accept the idea that one had necessarily to go through the four stages in order to attain freedom, or the ultimate fruit of life.

About the same time the *Bhagavadgītā* received its final form, Kauṭilya (circa 321–296 B.C.) wrote his *Arthaśāstra,* wherein he formulated a systematic utilitarian philosophy making use of the above-mentioned theory of the four stages of life as well as the conception of "the fruits of life."

It was no easy task for Kauṭilya to propound a teleological utilitarian moral theory highlighting the fruits of the mundane life in a context in which the *Vedas,* during a period of more than ten centuries, had come to assume unquestioned authority as revealed word. In fact, it was the strong belief that the *Vedas* represent a revelation and that the caste system was of divine origin that enabled the *Bhagavadgītā* to propound its deontological moral theory. Furthermore, this religious deontology rejected mundane concerns as being evil and called upon all persons in every walk of life to practice absolute self-sacrifice and renounce every fruit of action. In that context, presenting a utilitarian view emphasizing the fruits or consequences of action was not only a difficult but an unpopular task as well.

Unlike the Buddha, who openly condemned some of the Brahmanical beliefs, especially the authoritativeness of the *Vedas,* Kauṭilya worked within the Brahmanical framework. This is evident from his views about the nature and value of the sciences. He recognized four sciences:

1. Epistemology *(ānvīkṣikī)*
2. The triple *Vedas*
3. Economics, or more specifically the science relating to the productive professions such as agriculture, cattle breeding, and trade *(vārtā)*
4. Political science, or the science of government *(daṇḍa-nīti)*[24]

Kauṭilya needed to rescue a tradition totally immersed in religious deontology and bring it into this world of flesh and blood. This he could achieve only by injecting a dose of materialistic thinking; hence, his description of epistemology as consisting of two standpoints, namely the Brahmanical spiritualistic political philosophy (that is, the school of Manu [primodial man, according to Brahmanism]) and the materialistic political philosophy (that is, the school of Bṛhaspati).[25] Thus, epistemological inquiry includes the philosophies of Sāṅkhya (the deductive or a priori rational method), Yoga (the empirical method of the yogin who rejected sense experience)—both of which are recognized in the *Bhagavadgītā*—and Lokāyata (the materialistic empiricism that recognized sense experience and denied the validity of yogic intuition).[26] Kauṭilya probably felt that this synthesized epistemology would appeal to the spiritualist as well as the materialist, and for this reason considered it the prime science assigning a secondary place to the *Vedas.* Being a strategist, rather than a totally independent thinker, he was willing to recognize the *Vedas* as a science, whereas the revolutionary Buddha rejected the *Vedas,* replacing them with threefold knowledge.[27] Commenting on the value of each science, Kauṭilya states:

> Righteous and unrighteous acts *(dharmādharmau)* are learnt from the triple *Vedas;* wealth and no-wealth from *vārtā;* the expedient and the non-expedient *(nayānayau)* as well as potency and impotency *(balābale)* from the science of government.
>
> When seen in the light of these sciences, the science of Anviksiki is most beneficial for the world, keeps the mind steady and firm in weal and woe alike, and bestows excellence of foresight, speech and action.[28]

The philosophical significance of this analysis of the sciences should be evident when we consider the two forms of utlitarianism presented by Bentham and Mill in the Western world. Bentham's conception of utility as the happiness derived from the satisfaction of the five senses, which could then be formulated in terms of a hedonic calculus, is rather materialistic in temper. This was abandoned by Mill, who argued for a more enlightened form of utilitarianism that recognized the aesthetic component of experience as well, embodied in a statement such as "Socrates dissatisfied is better than a pig satisfied." Kauṭilya was hoping that the recognition of the usefulness of the *Vedas* would place his form of utilitarianism on a moral foundation.

The importance of the material conditions of life, downplayed in religious deontological ethics, is highlighted by Kauṭilya. Agriculture, cattle breeding, and trade, included under the science of *vārtā,* constituted the backbone of this agricultural economy. Without a strong economy and a constant flow of revenue into the treasury there cannot be good government. "It is by means of the treasury and the army obtained solely through Vārtā that the king can hold under his control both his and his enemy's party."[29] With this Kauṭilya arrives at the most important part of his dissertation. According to him, epistemological investigations, the triple *Vedas,* and the material conditions of life depend upon how the legal system works. His term for the science of government is *daṇḍa-nīti* (literally, punishment and law, or the laws of punishment). Even though punishment is underscored, it signifies something more than the mere prevention of crime; "it is a means to make acquisitions, to keep them secure, to improve them, and to distribute among the *deserved* the profits of improvement."[30] Kauṭilya believed that the progress of the entire world depends on this science of government.[31]

Interestingly, Kauṭilya emphasizes some form of welfare system, for indeed *artha* means both "wealth" and "welfare." Yet the welfare system does not involve equal treatment of all those who are in need, but only those that are deserving. How does one go about deciding eligibility for welfare? Kauṭilya does not address this question. The doctrine of karma was probably at the back of Kauṭilya's mind, even though he does not specifically state this.

Unlike the *Bhagavadgītā,* which encouraged the total withdrawal of the sense faculties because it distrusted the information derived from sense experience and highlighted yogic intuition as the ultimate source of knowledge, Kauṭilya, coming after the Buddha, who rejected the validity of a nonsensuous intuition, argued (as did the Buddha) for the restraint of excessive emotions instead of shutting off the sense faculties. Kauṭilya states, "Restraint of the organs of sense, on which success in study and discipline depends, can be enforced by abandoning lust, anger, greed, vanity, haughtiness and overjoy."[32]

This is the most important aspect of the Indian version of utilitarianism. Even if a person did not follow the four stages of life to its ultimate perfection, that is, if that person were to remain as a householder without renouncing the home life, his enjoyment of the material conditions of life still were restrained by the moral conditions widely accepted in society. Thus, even though Kauṭilya earned the dishonorific title of Machiavelli of the East, his utilitarianism was based on the traditional Indian values that emphasized the restraint of greed, hatred, vanity, and so on. Indeed, utilitarianism could not give rise to a capitalist economic system as it did in the West primarily because of this emphasis on restraint. For example, Kauṭilya was not advocating a philosophy comparable to that of the most influential economist of the Western world, namely, Lord Keynes, who, during the economic depression of the 1930s, argued that "For another hundred years we must pretend ourselves and to everyone that fair is foul and foul is fair; for foul is useful and fair is not. Avarice and usury and precaution must be our gods for a little longer still. For only they can lead us out of the tunnel of economic necessity into daylight."[33]

Having established utilitarian thought on a moral foundation, Kauṭilya, like his Western counterpart, Mill, tried to reconcile the deontology and utilitarianism. After enumerating the duties of the four castes as well as the four stages of life, he outlined the duties common to all:

> Harmlessness, truthfulness, purity, freedom from spite, abstinence from cruelty, and forgiveness are duties common to all.
>
> The observance of one's own duty leads one to Svarga and infinite bliss (Anantya). And when it is violated, the world will come to an end owing to confusion of castes and duties.
>
> Hence the king shall never allow people to swerve from their duties; for whoever upholds his own duty, ever adhering to the customs of the Aryas, and following the rules of caste and divisions of religious life, will surely be happy both here and hereafter.[34]

In the context of the age-old Brahmanical tradition, this is not a total revolution in moral philosophy. It is an attempt to defuse religious deontology, which was gaining momentum with the compilation of the *Bhagavadgītā.*

It is interesting that Kauṭilya, who picked up Brahmanical as well as the non-Brahmanical ideas and weaved them into an extremely sophisticated theory of monarchy and political philosophy, utilized it to dethrone the Nanda dynasty and to enthrone the Mauryan Candragupta. It is also possible to surmise that the Kālinga War demonstrated the regrettable aspects of his utilitarianism and compelled Candragupta's grandson, the famous Aśoka, to renounce that philosophy and embrace the compassionate teaching of the Buddha, with its humane and pragmatic moral philosophy.

Even though Kauṭilya's utilitarianism and the Buddha's pragmatism may have similarities, as did their Western counterparts, since Kauṭilya attempted to synthesize the ideas of the Brahmanical and the ascetic traditions, and seems to have implicitly recognized the celestial/terrestrial distinction explicit in the Brahmanical thought, his moral philosophy turned out to be very different from that of the Buddha. In fact, that very distinction is implicit in the utilitarian and pragmatic moral theories even of the Western world. The Buddha's moral pragmatism turns out to be rather unique for this reason.

Amoralism

In addition to the deontological and utilitarian traditions in ethics, the period preceding the Buddha also witnessed the emergence of a group of philosophers within the ascetic tradition who openly revolted against the Brahmanical metaphysical and ethical theories and advocated some form of amoralism. Some questioned the validity or utility of moral discourse by arguing in favor of materialism. Others refrained from any discussion of moral issues because they were reluctant to assert any notion of a human will, which by this time had been reduced to the extremely metaphysical conception of self *(ātma)* in the Brahmanical tradition. They utilized a theory of biological determinism in order to counter the Brahmanical moral conceptions.

Ajita Kesakambali

The most prominent materialist in ancient India was Ajita Kesakambali. The earliest reference to his school of thought is in the Buddha's *Discourse on the Fruits of Recluseship (Sāmaññaphala-suttanta).*[35] His ideas are discussed along with those of five other heterdox teachers, including the leader of Jainism, who was a senior contemporary of the Buddha. The discourse focuses more on Ajita's denial of the efficacy of moral discourse than on his materialism. He was totally opposed to those who believed that anything other than matter exists. He refers to them as *atthikavādin*, or "existentialist". According to him, these existentialists recognized generosity *(dāna)*, prayers *(yiṭṭha)*, rituals *(huta)*, the fruits of good and bad actions *(kamma)*, this world *(idha loka)*, the hereafter *(para loka)*, the concepts of mother and father (which introduce moral obligations in most societies), the belief in beings of spontaneous birth (i.e., gods, *sattā opapātikā*), and even the claims that the ascetics and brahmans lived in harmony, were well behaved, and knew this world as well as the next.[36] Ajita denied all these. Hence, he was looked upon as a nihilist *(natthika-vādin)*.

In many ways he compares well with the positivists of the modern world, who were reacting to the extremes in religious ideologies and social mores. Of course, Ajita needed an argument to justify his claims. This is where his materialism appears. His materialism was not the result of the study of the physical world and the laws that govern it, as is the case with modern science. Instead, his materialism was based upon his attempt to understand the human in the context of Brahmanical thought, with its extremist spiritualistic and social philosophy.

> This human person consists of the four great elements. When he dies, the solidity returns to the body of earth, fluidity to the body of water, caloric to the body of heat, and viscocity to the body of air.[37]

Ajita is indeed aware that there is something within the human that cannot be explained in terms of the four primary elements. He seems to have recognized a difference between dead matter and living cells, a fact that some modern scientists, such as Barry Commoner, would admit.[38] He needed an explanation that would not upset his materialist thesis, hence his statement, "The faculties return to space" *(ākāsaṃ indriyāni saṃkamanti)*.[39]

After this analysis of the human, Ajita returns to his main thesis:

> Ideas like generosity are simply the conceptualizations of a stupid person *(dattu-paññatti)*. He who speaks of their existence, his words are empty, confused and a cry of desperation *(tesaṃ tucchaṃ musā vilāpo ye keci atthikavādaṃ vadanti)*.[40]

His first name, Ajita, means the "unconquered," and the second, Kesa-kambali, implies "one who wears a robe of human hair." The latter indicates that he was a practitioner of austerities. This means that, while being an ascetic, which would also mean that he was not a materialist given to pleasures of sense, Ajita was simply condemning the metaphysical foundations of the Brahmanical moral theory predominant at this time. In fact, Ajita's views are not very different from those of some of the modern-day philosophers of science who by any standard could be considered good people but who advocate materialism primarily because of the metaphysics involved in ethical discourse. Like the latter, Ajita seems to have been very argumentative, hence his name, "the unconquered."

Pūraṇa Kassapa

Pūraṇa Kassapa, whose ideas resemble those of Ajita, denied the accruing of merit *(puñña)* or demerit *(pāpa)* on the basis of good or bad actions, respectively. According to him, taking life, stealing, unchastity, or lying do not bring about demerit. There would be no accumulation of demerit if one were to reduce all the living beings on this earth to a pile of flesh. If one were to walk the southern bank of the river Ganges, killing whatever beings one came across, one would not accumulate any demerit. Similarly, if one were to traverse the northern bank, practicing charity or praying and promoting others to do the same, one would not pile up any merit. Charity, self-control, restraint, and truthfulness are ineffective.

Unlike Ajita, Pūraṇa provides no reasons or a metaphysical position to justify such condemnation. The only clue to an understanding of his amoralism is his use of the terms merit and demerit. It may be noted that the Buddha, who came after Pūraṇa, made a distinction between merit and demerit on the one hand, and good *(kusala)* and bad *(akusala)* on the other. For the sake of the unenlightened, he allowed the idea that merit and demerit can be accumulated. However, the enlightened one, he maintained, is one who has renounced the ideas of merit and demerit *(puññapāpapahīṇa)*,[41] although not the concepts of good and bad. Promoting good *(kusalassa upasampadā)* was part of the ultimate teachings of the Buddha.[42]

It is clear that the Buddha allowed the concepts of merit and demerit only as incentives for the unenlightened person to adopt a moral life. But the idea of accumulation was not one that could eventually lead to freedom from bondage. As the Buddhist text reports, Pūraṇa did not make this distinction. As such, his interest seems to be in totally condemning the Brahmanical and Jaina notions of accumulation of merit for salvific purposes, and then offering no alternative. Furthermore, it may be noted that Pūraṇa used the term *kiriya* instead of *kamma* to refer to action, and this term was the one employed by the Jainas.

Pakudha Kaccāyana

Pakudha Kaccāyana's amoralism is different from both Ajita's and Pūraṇa's. The thrust of his argument is in the direction of denying a "person," again prompted by the Brahmanical conception of self. Yet his denial of self is not comparable to that of Ajita, who reduced the human to the five material substances. Pakudha speaks of seven substances: the four material elements, happiness *(sukha)*, pain *(dukkha)*, and the life principle *(jiva)*.[43] His is more an essentialist enterprise that recognizes irreducible elements, both physical and psychic. He is an amoralist because he takes the elements to be permanent, eternal, uncreated, and noncreative. Therefore, "even if one were to behead a person, one is not depriving that person of his life, but is simply creating some space between the seven elements with a knife."[44]

Makkhali Gosāla

Makkhali Gosāla, the leader of the band of wandering ascetics called Ājīvikas, is philosophically the most sophisticated among these amoralists. He presented a carefully worked out theory of biological determinism that, to some extent, influenced the Jainas. Makkhali believed that beings are conditioned by three factors only: fate *(niyati)*, species *(saṅgati)*, and self-nature *(bhāva = svabhāva)*.[45] The initial condition that determines how and why a living being comes to belong to any specific species remains a mystery. It is simply predetermination. Once it appears in a particular species, a species being a harmonious concomitance of a group of characteristics, then it behaves according to the nature of that species.

Makkhali's primary interest is in denying the efficacy of the will. Interestingly, he does not reject the concepts of purity *(visuddhi)* or impurity *(saṃkilesa)*. He simply does not want to recognize the activity of the self *(atta-kāra)* or the activity of the human *(purisa-kāra)* in the attainment of purity or impurity. But to what does purity and impurity belong? It seems that they are part and parcel of the mysterious conditions that determine the life of beings; they are part of biology. Hence, beings continue to evolve in the cycle of existences *(saṃsāra)* and, after some incalculable period of time, automatically reach the end of their suffering. The idea that virtues and rituals, austerities and the moral life could bring about a change in one's life or bring to fruition the latent karmic tendencies was not acceptable to Makkhali.[46]

Here again we find a member of the ascetic tradition unwilling to recognize two metaphysical views associated with ethical discussions, namely, the concept of the will and the idea of potentiality. Yet he did not abandon the age-old distinction between the transcendental and the phenomenal, the celestial and the terrestrial, for predermination, species, and self-nature, as well as purity and impurity, are part of the transcendental or the celestial, while the being itself, the content, is phenomenal or terrestrial. It is not surprising that the later Indian theistic philosophers utilized Makkhali's system of thinking to introduce the concept of God *(īśvara)*.[47]

Mahāvīra and Jainism

While the teachings of the four heterodox teachers who propounded some form of amoralism did not survive long, the doctrines of Mahāvīra (and his predecessor, Pārśvanātha), popularly known as Jainism, have remained a significant philosophical and religious alternative to Brahmanism until today. It is interesting to note that Jainism survived while the more popular Buddhist tradition was almost completely extinct by the tenth century A.D. One reason for the survival of Jainism and the extinction of Buddhism in India, in spite of Buddhism being a part of the ascetic tradition, is that Jainism was less radical and more syncretic in its doctrinal content than Buddhism, which rejected many of the foundational theories of Brahmanism. Another reason for Jainism's survival is its willingness to develop its own religious rituals associated with the birth of a child, a marriage, and the like. Buddhism did not get involved in such matters.

Mahāvīra is the systematizer of Jaina thought. As mentioned earlier, the four philosophers who advocated some form of amoralism did so primarily because they were compelled to deny the efficacy of human effort as well as free will when opposing the metaphysical notion of self of the Brahmanical thinkers. It is precisely this situation that Mahāvīra wanted to avoid. Being a syncretic thinker, he saw no difficulty in accepting the concept of a permanent self as well as other requirements for a moral philosophy, such as the concepts of human effort and free will. Of the *ātma/brahma* duo of Brahmanism, Mahāvīra could recognize the objectivity of *ātma* but not of *brahma,* for the latter, as explained earlier, was the foundation of the caste system and its duties, which were rejected by the early ascetic tradition and which relied upon the theory of the stages of life. Furthermore, after adopting the biological determinism of the Ājīvikas, Mahāvīra needed an equally strong conception of human effort and free will. The conception of action, *kiriya,* rid of its association with caste, performed this function and became the central conception of Jainism.

The central role accorded to action allows Jainism to have a theory of morals. Hence it is referred to as a *kiriyavāda,* in contrast to the four theories of amoralism *(akiriyavāda)* discussed earlier. In fact, even though the Buddha was critical of the metaphysical views as well as the moral theory of the Jainas, he is said to have made special concessions to the Jaina disciples who were converted to Buddhism, especially in regard to the rules of monastic discipline, primarily because they were considered to be *kiriyavādins.*[48] However, Jaina and Buddhist theories differ from one another in some important respects. As I pointed out elsewhere,[49] Mahāvīra wanted his theory of action to be objective in an ultimate sense so that it could be on par with the theory of biological determinism that he borrowed from the Ājīvikas. In contrast, the Buddha, not being committed to this form of objectivity, laid emphasis on a psychological analysis of human action.

Biological determinism, in addition to being a response to a a philosopher's call for objectivity, was also an answer to his appeal for clarity and certainty, both of which militate against a psychological analysis of human action. Determinism implies the knowability of connections between events with almost absolute certainty. An element of uncertainty would undermine a theory of determinism. Psychology has often been considered the spoiler of such discourse.

In his attempt to render his theory of human action compatible with his adopted biological determinism, Mahāvīra was compelled to present a theory of knowledge unique to Indian philosophy. It is generally held that he was a nonabsolutist. However, this nonabsolutism was an attempt to accommodate the ordinary empirical modes of knowing. It consists of a theory of predication that admits seven possibilities *(syādvāda)* and a theory of seven modes of explanation *(naya)*.[50] Whether these were presented in the very form in which they are explained by the later commentators is not certain. However, they represent the essence of Mahāvīra's epistemology, which is compatible with his metaphysics as well as his ethics.

In a theory that is relativist in the extreme, there cannot be any error, for every imaginable possibility seems to have been taken care of. Yet time and again unpredicted and unanticipated situations occur even if they are to be of minimal significance. There is one simple solution to this epistemological quandary: the claim to omniscience on the part of one who really knows. It is therefore not surprising that Mahāvīra had to claim omniscience *(sarvajñatā)* (he being the first human being in history to have claimed it), whereas other theological traditions placed in comparable situations attributed such omniscience to divinity. Mahāvīra's theory of action has to be evaluated in the context of this theory of knowledge. Any other method would do violence to it.

First, the actions under consideration have to satisfy the requirement of objectivity. If the criterion of objectivity is public verification, the mental actions of a person would be excluded, for they are not publicly observable. If, on the other hand, we place objectivity within the context of the individual, mental actions definitely would be objective. If not for such objectivity, the suprarationalist of the modern Western world, René Descartes, could not take one step forward in establishing his rationalist philosophy. Mahāvīra, being a contemplative of the ascetic tradition, had no difficulty in recognizing the objective validity of mental acts, even though he was unwilling to delve into the psychological springs of mental, verbal, and bodily actions, as the Buddha did.

Thus, to start with, Mahāvīra admitted three forms of action: bodily, verbal, and mental. The reality and objectivity of experienced events or actions performed may be asserted as long as they are taken in themselves, that is, known as they are. The moment someone engages in the archeology of knowledge, that reality and objectivity begin to get blurred and fuzzy. For this reason, in the understanding and explanation of the three types of action, Mahāvīra was unwilling to make any inquiries into the nature of the action, the background in which it is performed, or the motivations for such action. For him an action is an action regardless of whether it is performed with or without intention. This enabled him to formulate a one-to-one relationship between action and consequence, for there could not be a situation where the same action would lead to two different results. It also helped him to simplify the problem of responsibility. For example, if two persons were to commit two different homicides, one intentionally and the other unintentionally, under normal situations the former would be held responsible and the latter could go free. The strict determinism that Mahāvīra espoused would break down at this point. Furthermore, it is possible that even the person who intentionally commits murder may be under a delusion, a hallucination, or some other mental disease delimiting his capacity for reasoning. For Mahāvīra, this too could not be a mitigating factor, for it involves error on the part of the murderer. These two aspects of Mahāvīra's doctrine of action, namely, the strictly determined relationship between action and consequence and the possibility of knowing this relationship without error, are clearly reflected in the following statement of one of his disciples who argued with a Buddhist.

> If a savage puts a man on a spit and roasts him, mistaking him for a fragment of the granary; or a baby, mistaking him for a gourd, he will not be guilty of murder! . . . If anybody thrusts a spit through a man or a baby, mistaking him for a fragment of the granary, puts him on the fire and roasts him, that will be a meal fit for the Buddhas to breakfast upon. . . . Well-controlled men cannot accept your denial of guilt incurred by [unintentional] doing harm to human beings. . . . It is impossible to mistake a fragment of the granary for a man; only an unworthy man can say it.[51]

An offshoot of this theory of action is absolute nonviolence *(ahiṃsā)*, which the more traditional disciples practice even to this day. Sweeping the ground on which one has to walk, drinking filtered water, and covering the mouth and nose with a cloth through fear that one would be destroying life imperceptible to the naked eye are some of the extreme practices that developed out of this doctrine of nonviolence.

Strict determinism associated with Mahāvīra's doctrine of action generated other problems as well, the most important involving the concept of ultimate freedom *(nirvāṇa)*. As stated earlier, Mahāvīra's contemporaries in the ascetic tradition denied human effort and free will, the exception being Makkhali, the Ājīvika, who, while denying human effort and free will, did admit some form of ultimate freedom. Mahāvīra's was an attempt to accommodate all three—determinism, free will, and ultimate freedom. He did so in a manner very consistent with his epistemology and metaphysics.

In order to render the consequences of action as real and objective as the actions themselves that produced them, Mahāvīra conceived of these consequences as fine material particles generated by the actions. According to him, the human soul *(jīva)*, originally pure and luminous, comes to be gradually covered by the adventitious karmic particles. The process of purifying the soul therefore consists of two kinds of activity, one directed at getting rid of the already accumulated particles and the other intended to prevent the influx of new particles. Since the consequences of action are not variable, that is, a particular act always carries the same consequence, consequence is synonymous with punishment *(daṇḍa)*. Thus, the accumulation of karmic particles would mean the storing up of an invariable series of punishments to be faced in the future, and if these punishments are allowed to take their natural course, a human will have created an endless series of existences for himself or herself. However, it is possible for one to accelerate that process by bringing upon oneself some punishment to offset future punishments. Practice of severe austerity *(tapas)* is intended to achieve this. At the same time it is necessary to prevent further accumulation of karmic particles. This is achieved through nonaction *(akaraṇa)*. In Mahāvīra's perception, the ability to undertake these two activities constitutes human effort and free will. While the first activity led the Jainas to the practice of severe austerities, the second in its extreme form contributed to fasting, for this is the ultimate form of nonaction. Thus, death by fasting became an ideal, and it was achieved by Mahāvīra. It may be considered the culmination of the practice of the fourth stage of life, the stage of *saṃnyāsin*.

The moral life recommended for the lay person does not have the same austereness. Yet the principle of nonviolence is binding upon the householder, especially when they choose their vocations. As trade or commerce was one such vocation of nonviolence, it is not surprising that many Jainas who took their religion seriously were traditionally merchants.

Despite being nontheistic, Jainism contributed to the distinction between the transcendent and the empirical, the celestial and the terrestrial. This is because it recognized a sphere that is more stable and permanent, both in biology and in human activity, and assumed the possibility of error-free knowledge relegating the senses to a lower level as being unreliable and untrustworthy. Therefore, its moral philosophy could not escape the sacred-secular dichotomy. This is the similarity between Brahmanism and Jainism and, as mentioned earlier, one of the reasons for Jainism's survival alongside Brahmanism.

CHAPTER 2

Knowledge

THE BUDDHA was born and bred in the Brahmanical tradition. As the prince of the Sakyans, he was in a position to receive the best education anyone during his day could get. He was well educated in the traditional system of learning—the Vedic literature, its philosophical content, as well as the ancillary sciences *(vedāṅga)*. As is evident from his discourses, he was a sophisticated linguist. It was his disillusionment with the thought and practices of the Brahmanical tradition that led him to abandon his regal responsibilities and devote his life to the pursuit of what he called the good *(kusala)* and the noble path of peace *(santivarapadaṃ)*.[1] The metaphorical presentation of this disillusionment is found in the later Buddhist tradition in its very popular anecdote.[2] At this time the only alternative to the the Brahmanical tradition was asceticism, hence the Buddha's renunciation of the household life in order to test the promises of asceticism to deal with human problems. However, he was not a blind follower of this mode of life. At the end of six years of experimentation with extreme forms of asceticism, he was on the verge of death. It may be remembered that on a later occasion his contemporary, Mahāvīra, actually succumbed to death, considering it the highest ideal. Not gaining any new insights into the good and the peaceful through such severe austerities, the Buddha gradually regained his health and devoted himself to contemplation. Unfortunately, the nature of this contemplation and the sort of information it yielded have generally been understood in relation to the ideas prevalent in the Brahmanical as well as the ascetic traditions, that is, *the very systems of thought the Buddha rejected.*

It would be appropriate to recount the basic epistemological commitments of the Buddha's predecessors and then proceed to examine the reasons for his rejection of them.

First and foremost is the idea that behind the empirical world of change and impermanence is a sphere of the incorruptible, the permanent, and the unchanging. According to some of the Buddha's predecessors, this is true of the objective world only; for others it is true of both the subject and the object; and for still others it is true not only of the subject and the object but also of morals. What is significant is that most philosophers who contributed to one or the other of these theories considered full-fledged sense experience (i.e., sense experience that includes the activity of the mind as well) as an inadequate source of knowledge. The materialists who admitted an incorruptible material or physical reality, while accepting the validity of the five physical senses only, depended heavily on deductive reasoning to establish their point of view. Those who believed in the permanence of both the objective and subjective spheres, as well as those who believed in the incorruptibility of the moral law, were compelled either to accept the dictates of deductive reasoning or admit a transcendental intuition. They were the Brahmanical philosophers. Jaina Mahāvīra, with a similar commitment, fell back on omniscience. Contrary to the popular belief that in all these cases epistemology preceded metaphysics, our analysis of pre-Buddhist background makes it clear that metaphysics provided a justification for epistemology.

For this reason, the Buddha, who was searching for the good and the peaceful and who was dissatisfied with the claims of the Brahmanical as well as the ascetic traditions, was compelled to examine the epistemological claims of these traditions and see whether they revealed what these philosophers considered to be truth and reality. His epistemological discoveries, which he considered unprecedented in the Indian context, describing them as "the arising of vision, of knowledge, of insight and of illumination regarding phenomena unheard of before" *(pubbe ananussutesu dhammesu cakkhuṃ udapādi vijjā udapādi ñāṇaṃ udapādi āloko udapādi),* need serious consideration. His statement about his discoveries is not an exaggeration on the part of a swollen head, but a paean of joy *(udāna),* a statement of confidence or a "lion's roar" *(sīhanāda)* of someone who, after unbelievable sacrifices, came to realize the nature of existence and how to deal with it.

Let us first examine the interpretation of the Buddha's epistemological standpoint by some of the modern interpreters. It is assumed that the Buddha's contemplation followed the lines already carved out by pre-

Buddhist contemplatives like Ālāra Kālāma and Uddaka Rāmaputta and that it was only a one-step advancement. This would mean that he simply improved upon the existing contemplative or yogic tradition. If that were the case, then the information he gained through this advancement ought to relate to the very same thing that the pre-Buddhist contemplatives were trying to understand, namely, the permanent and eternal foundation of human existence. Matters were further complicated as a result of his statement

> So I, monks, being myself liable to birth, . . . decay, . . . disease, . . . death, . . . sorrow, . . . defilement, having known peril in what is liable to birth, . . . decay, . . . disease, . . . death, . . . sorrow, . . . defilement, seeking the not-born, . . . the non-decaying, . . . the non-disease, . . . the non-mortal, . . . the non-sorrow, . . . the non-defiled, realized the not-born, . . . the non-decaying, . . . the non-disease, . . . the non-mortal, . . . the non-sorrow, . . . the non-defiled freedom *(nibbāna)*, incomparable release from bondage.[3]

Even when the Buddha had not used the terms permanent and eternal, some who read this and similar passages did not hesitate to reach the conclusion that here is the permanent and eternal foundation of existence, here is the celestial, the ultimate ground of the terrestrial. The statement that follows should have prevented them from coming to such a conclusion. It reads, "Knowledge and insight arose in me: 'unshakable is my freedom; this is my last birth; now there will be no future becoming.' "[4]

Understood in the context of this latter statement, the former statement refers to *what he has achieved in this life.* To an ordinary person or even to an intellectual, this claim would be frightening because he or she would not want this to be the last life. For the Buddha, the overcoming of birth, decay, disease, death, sorrow, and defilement is to be achieved simply by *not* being born in the future, that is, by not having the *conditions* that lead to rebirth and rebecoming *(apunabbhava)*.[5] Among the various conditions that lead to rebirth and rebecoming are craving for becoming *(bhava-taṇhā)* (i.e., becoming more and more of what one is or retaining one's identity without change) and the craving for becoming someone different *(vibhava-taṇhā)* (i.e., reaching out for a totally different form of existence).[6]

For these reasons, immediately after stating what he has achieved as compared to his quests before enlightenment, the Buddha proceeds to explain the content of his knowledge.

> This fact, which is difficult to perceive, difficult to comprehend, peaceful, delightful, not given to *a priori* reasoning, effective and to be experienced by the wise, was realized by me. These people are delighting in attachment, engrossed in attachment, nourished by attachment. By these people, who are delighting in attachment, engrossed in attachment and nourished by attachment, this standpoint, namely, conditionality *(idappaccayatā)*, dependent arising *(paṭiccasamuppādo)*, is perceived with difficulty.[7]

Conditionality, dependent arising—this is what existence is, if one can speak of existence. There is no indication whatsoever that there is something beyond conditionality, something that is absolutely independent. Independence, or autonomy (to use a Kantian phrase), is a purely substantialist or transcendentalist conception. Freedom is not absolute independence *(appaṭiccasamuppāda)*. As such, for those who are delighting in attachment, engrossed in attachment, nourished by attachment, even the state of freedom that the Buddha achieved, which is the appeasement of all dispositions *(sabbasaṅkhārasamatha)*, relinquishing of all grasping *(sabbūpadhipaṭinissagga)*, waning of craving *(taṇhakkhaya)*, dispassion *(virāga)*, and cessation *(nirodha)*, is also not easily perceived.[8]

If this is what the Buddha achieved with the attainment of enlightenment, and if this is the content of that enlightenment, as recorded in one of the most authentic discourses, *Discourse on the Noble Quest (Ariyapariyesana-sutta)*, then his theory of knowledge has to be different from what was found in the Indian philosophical tradition before him. It was not an advancement on what was already there. It was something new. The attainment involves not the transcendence of sensory experience, but the appeasement of dispositions, relinquishing of grasping, waning of craving, and so on. There is no statement whatsoever that would indicate such transcendence or abandoning of sense experience in favor of a nonsensuous intuition. Furthermore, the content of that knowledge, namely, conditionality or dependent arising, also does not require the elimination of sense experience. Those that are eliminated are the very conditions that contribute to the belief in permanence and the metaphysical postulates justifying permanence. If impermanence is what all life is about, it is what is evident to the unprejudiced sense experience. The Buddha's description of the restraint of the senses *(indriya-saṃvara)* reads as follows:

> Herein, . . . , a monk, having seen a visible object with the eye, does not grasp on to a mysterious substance *(nimitta)* and qualities *(anuvyañjana)*. When the faculty under consideration remains unrestrained, there would be the influx of coveteousness, discontent as well as evil and unwholesome tendencies; so he undertakes to restrain it, he protects the faculty of the eye, he achieves the restraint of the eye.[9]

It is clear from this analysis that evil and unwholesome tendencies occur as a result of the pursuit of metaphysical postulates such as substances and qualities in the objects perceived. Thus, with the elimination of unwholesome tendencies like attachment and aversion, which is freedom, a person tends to abandon the pursuit of permanence, substances being permanent entities postulated in order to solve the metaphysical problems caused by the reduction of objects into qualities.

In the modern Western world, the analysis of an object of experience into substance and qualities is what triggered at least two centuries of controversy among the empiricists. David Hume's denial of substance and his reduction of experience into atomic impressions brought about the Kantian "Copernican revolution," which introduced the so-called transcendental categories. More recently, Western philosophers have come to realize the futility as well as the dangers of this whole enterprise.[10]

A Western critic of Buddhism may raise the question, How could the Buddha, living during the sixth century B.C. in India, advise his disciples not to go looking for substances and qualities on occasions of sense experience? Isn't this reading too much into the rather primitive Buddhist texts? The answer is simple. Substantialism and transcendence, in the more sophisticated form in which they appeared in the Western world, were rampant in the pre-Buddhist Indian background. In fact, the realization of nonsubstantiality *(anatta)* of all phenomena was the outcome of the Buddha's pursuit of the yogic contemplation to its climax, namely the attainment of the cessation of perception and what is felt *(saññāvedayitanirodha)*. Indeed, it is the one step he took beyond the four higher stages of contemplation achieved by his predecessors. While his predecessors assumed they had reached a perception of reality beyond description, the extra step taken by the Buddha enabled him to realize that the content of perception is empty of any substance.

It is after this realization that the Buddha turned his attention to the problem of knowledge. If yogic contemplation did not lead to a transcendent intuition, there was no justification for recognizing objects that are beyond sense experience, objects such as permanent and eternal selves in the subject and similarly permanent and enduring susbtances *(ātma = svabhāva)* in the world of objects. He also realized that such a search undergirded the pre-Buddhist understanding of both yogic contemplation and sense experience. The reason for this, according to him, was human anxiety *(paritassanā)*.[11] The Buddha was therefore not prepared to fault either yogic contemplation or sense experience. Instead he was ready to accept both without tainting them with a search for permanence. I have already presented fairly comprehensive analyses of these two sources of knowledge, which need not be repeated here.[12] What is important is that the Buddha's explanation of these two sources gives no indication whatsoever that they provide information about anything permanent and eternal. Also, his explanation does not allow room for an essentialist interpretation, which is another passion on the part of the reflective thinkers, that is, to understand an experienced event "as it is" without reference to the background in which it occurs.

Thus, the Buddha's formulation of the nature of existence as conditionality or dependent arising carefully avoids this twofold passion: passion for permanence and passion for essence. This is achieved through an empirical understanding of phenomena in a historical present, or what may be characterized as "radical empiricism." In this most important philosophical issue, the Buddha, the linguist, realized that the current vocabulary did not allow him to express his idea of the historical present. The term *vartamāna* simply meant "existing," with no implication of any relationship to the past. Therefore, on the analogy of the term he had already coined to express his central conception, namely, "dependent arising" *(paṭiccasamuppāda)*, he created the term *paccuppanna*, meaning "that which has arisen dependent upon," which expresses the idea of the present related to the immediate past. This is what the radical empiricist of the Western world, William James, referred to as the "specious present."[13] The historical context is not fixed by any definite parameters or horizons. It is variable depending on how much information about the event can be gathered. These horizons thus can contract and expand, and such contraction and expansion comes to be embodied in the very conceptual apparatus that is being used to explain these horizons. This understanding is expressed by the phrase *yathābhūta-ñāṇa*, "knowledge of the manner in which things have come to be."

Taking the information provided by the higher forms of knowledge as well as sense experience in the above manner, the Buddha was able to formulate general principles according to which phenomena are said to occur. These general principles are neither absolute nor incorrigible. All that can be asserted about them is that they have been valid so far, and one should be prepared to revise them whenever new situations occur or new information is available. It is for this reason that the Buddha formulated the most general principle in the least specific language, that is, the language of dependence. Even after such a formulation, all he said about it was, "This status has remained [valid] so far" *(ṭhitā 'va sā dhātu)*.[14]

So much for empirical knowledge. Where empiricism was a weak claimant to knowledge of permanence and essence, rationalism has remained its most powerful proponent. Even in the Indian context, before the employment of yogic intuition as the source of the knowledge of *ātma* and *brahma*, deductive reasoning established their veracity. "Nothing comes out of nothing," was the a priori premise on which the "existent" *(sat)*, as the primeval ground of everything *(sarvam)*, was founded. Although logic as a science had not attained the same level of development that it reached during the medieval period, existence and nonexistence *(asat)* served as the basis of a two-valued logic *(tarka)* often utilized in debates among philosophers. It is with Sañjaya Bellaṭṭhiputta that we first come across a theory of four alternatives. But either because he was an absolute skeptic or was someone who believed in ineffability, he negated all four possibilities. This was followed by the Jaina theory of seven possibilities *(sapta-bhaṅgī-naya)*. It may be remembered that despite their recognition of seven possibilities *(syād)*, the ultimate goal of the Jainas was to account for every possibility so that nothing was left out; hence Mahāvīra's claim to omniscience *(sarvajñatā)*. For this reason, Jaina logic, though apparently relativistic and nonabsolutist, is ultimately absolutist.

The Buddha's radical nonsubstantialism or nonabsolutism called for a method of reasoning and a system of logic that was totally different from those of the pre-Buddhist thinkers.

He rejected *a priori,* or deductive, reasoning *(takka)* as being of little use in discovering truth, for its conclusions can be either true or false. One cannot reach any practical conclusion on the basis of such reasoning.[15] Instead, he relied upon *a posterior,* or inductive, reasoning. On the basis of observations confined to the historical present, that is, direct observations of features not strictly confined to a particular time or moment (*akālika,* which allows for universal features), he was able to make inferences into the past *(atīta)* and the future *(anāgata).*[16] The features not confined to a particular time refer to the relations among events. These relations are not separable from the events. He recognized empirically related events *(paṭiccasamuppanna dhamma).* However, for the sake of inference, this common relation needs to be highlighted. In presenting inductive inference in this manner he avoided the criticism that it involved circularity. These inferences are not absolute, but only guides that help us to deal with the future.

Logic in this nonsubstantialist epistemology avoided the age-old two-valued system. This again called for drastic changes not only in regard to the purpose of logical analysis, but also the terminology utilized. The sharp dichotomy between the true and the false had to be abandoned. Until this time the true *(satya)* had been identified with the existent and the false *(asatya)* with the nonexistent. This dichotomy could not function within the framework where nonsubstantiality and dependent arising were key concepts, the latter being founded on the experience of phenomena in the historical present. Thus, we find the use of a new set of terms expressive of this radical empiricism. The earlier term for truth, *sacca,* is retained, but its meaning is modified by the use of the term *bhūta,* "become", as its synonym.[17] The term *asacca,* which meant nonexistence, is dropped, and two new terms—*musā* and *abhūta*—used to express the idea of the false. They express two slightly different senses of the concept of the false. *Musā,* meaning "confusion," explains the false as being part of the epistemological problem. Since truth is not absolute, but dependent and conditional, it was necessary to allow for an element of doubt regarding its opposite, namely, the false, hence the definition of false as confusion. The term *abhūta,* "not become" (opposite of *bhūta* =

truth, become), leaves the problem at the ontological level. Even if one wants to conceive of the false as the nonexistent at the present time, the false as the "not become" allows for the possibility of the so-called false becoming true in the context of new situations or with the discovery of new conditions. The true and false, according to this definition, are *contraries* rather than *contradictories.*

This nonabsolutist definition of true and false left the Buddha with the following truth values:

$$\begin{aligned} p &= \text{true} \\ -p &= \text{confusion (contrary)} \\ (p \cdot -p) &= \text{confusion (contrary)} \end{aligned}$$

With this he was ready to deal a devastating blow to the absolutists who often resorted to the linguistic ineffability of truth. For him, the genuinely false is the fourth alternative,

$$-(p \cdot -p) = \text{false } (\textit{kali}) \text{ (contradiction).}$$[18]

In the eyes of one who has recognized the primacy of sense experience, this last alternative represents the collapse or destruction of epistemology, hence referred to as *kali* (epistemological sin).

This system of logic stands in complete contrast to the system that dominated Indian and Western philosophy for more than two thousand years. For example, the Western philosopher who first articulated in great detail this system of two-valued logic and also emphasized what is known as *araetic,* or virtue-based, ethics is Aristotle. The Buddha and Aristotle may be compared only to the extent that they were philosophers willing to recognize virtues as the foundation of moral life. However, the comparison ends here primarily because of Aristotle's epistemology, which did not allow him to recognize any moral principles. It is generally believed that Aristotle's reluctance to recognize moral laws or principles was the result of his rejection of the Platonic forms. Yet a careful analysis of his ideas in the *Nichomachean Ethics* would seem to indicate a different reason. Aristotle analyzed knowledge into two types corresponding to the two parts of the soul—the rational and the irrational.[19] The rational is "one by which we contemplate the kinds of things whose *originative causes are invariable,*" and the irrational is "one by which we contemplate *variable things* (emphasis added)."[20] The former is scientific, the latter calculative.

Speaking of scientific knowledge, Aristotle says

> We all suppose that what we know is not even capable of being otherwise; of things capable of being otherwise we do not know, when they have passed our observation, whether they exist or not. Therefore, the object of scientific knowledge is of necessity. Therefore it is eternal; for things that are of necessity in the unqualified sense are all eternal; and things that are eternal are ungenerated and imperishable.[21]

The calculative, while pointing a finger toward the rational or the scientific, deals with the variable, and this includes "both things made and things done."[22] "Things made" are represented by art and "things done" by morals. The pointing of the finger is no more than admitting the fact that neither aesthetics nor ethics can come close to the truths formulated in science and logic.

In contrast, the Buddha's epistemological standpoint allowed him to confine his philosophy to the world given to sensible experience as well as some of the higher forms of knowledge, such as telepathy and retrocognition, yielded by excessive concentration and the principles that function within that world without taking refuge in the permanent, the incorruptible, the celestial, or the Absolute.

It was mentioned at the very outset of this chapter that the Buddha renounced the household life and adopted asceticism because he was interested in what is good *(kusala)* and peaceful *(santi),* because he was not interested in discovering the permanent and eternal foundations of existence. For these reasons, in spite of his enormous involvement in epistemological inquiry, he did not abandon his major concern, namely the search for the good and the peaceful. Indeed, his epistemology was completely colored by such concerns. Therefore, for him, what is true is important only insofar as it is relevant to what is good. Any conception of truth not relevant to making human life wholesome and good would simply be metaphysical and therefore unedifying. The Buddha's view of metaphysics is thus different from that of the positivists of the Western world. For the positivists, metaphysics on the whole is meaningless because it does not come within the sphere of knowledge, this latter being defined in terms of positively identifiable objects. The positively identifiable objects are those given to the five physical senses. While the Buddha, as an empiricist, recognized the importance of the knowledge derived from the five physical senses,[23] he was not willing to confine knowledge to the sense faculties alone. For him, even knowledge derived from the senses could be metaphysical and hence meaningless if it had no relevance to human life. Questions relating to the extent and duration of the universe, which would absorb the attention even of the positivists, were laid aside by the Buddha because they did not in any way contribute to the welfare and happiness of living beings. Truths are important not in themselves but insofar as they are relevant to human life. He was not reluctant to assert that what is true is useful and that what is useful is true. However, usefulness is to be judged in terms of both the material *(attha)* and moral *(dhamma)* development of the human as well as the society in which that person lives.

CHAPTER 3

The Fact-Value Distinction

ONE OF THE MOST difficult problems a student of ethics, whether Eastern or Western, has to face is the royal pair of dichotomies, fact and value, that has haunted philosophers for centuries. Centuries before the rise of Buddhism, the Indian philosophers had made this distinction. As mentioned in Chapter 1, it appeared in the form of *ātma-brahma* dichotomy, soon to be unified under the more superior form, *brahma* (ultimate good), a move that was intended to establish the superiority of the brahman class. Similarly, we find the early rationalists of the Western world, especially Plato, making a tripartite division of reality into truth, beauty and goodness, and then unifying them under the concept of the supreme Good, though this was not intended for justifying the superiority of a social class. It may be noted that the early Indian dichotomy between fact and value was later developed into a tripartite division similar to Plato's when the Indian thinkers recognized *brahma* as the ultimate aesthetic experience *(rasa)* as well. In either case, the distinctions were not the result of any empirical knowledge, but the consequence of a search—the search for certainty. Empirical justification in the form of an intuition (in the Indian case, yogic intuition) was offered only after the search for certainty regarding ultimate facts and values had reached its culmination, the actual process by which that certainty was achieved being deductive.

The rationalist, or deductive, search for absolute certainty in the sphere of knowledge and understanding often tended to undermine the importance of the empirical world. The inability to ignore the concrete factual world, the world that impresses upon the conscious human with an "objective pull," with an irresistible feeling of clearness and vividness, provided the empiricist philosophers with a rationale for claiming certainty with regard to the brute facts of sensory experience, again creating an almost unbridgeable chasm between fact and value. For the empiricist, facts are the given, the real and the ultimate, and, therefore, amenable to clear and precise formulation in terms of invariable and verifiable laws, while values, being human fabrications or products of human convention, cannot be subjected to such strict formulations. The objectivity of facts and the subjectivity of values continued to be justified by the materialistically inclined empiricists, both classical and modern, Eastern and Western.

The recognition of the fact-value distinction and the rejection of values as part of the factual world have been carried out most aggressively in Western philosophy during the twentieth century. Logical Atomism, espoused by Bertrand Russell, and the Positivism of August Comte, with their cognitivist and verificationist theories of truth and reality based upon the scientific conception of what "exists," provided a foundation for the logical positivist's condemnation of ethics as being noncognitive and plainly emotive. These logical positivists were thus working within the framework of two irreconcilable concepts of truth. The first consisted of analytic truths of logic and mathematics, which are tautological. The second represented the synthetic and the empirical, which were defined as ideas that correspond to objective physical reality. Any idea that did not fall into one of these two watertight compartments was rejected as being metaphysical and meaningless. There was no room for a third kind of truth, such as the pragmatic. Moral discourse, according to this definition of truth, was no more than an expression of emotion and was without positive philosophical content.

Although emotivism in ethics is generally looked upon as a twentieth-century phenomenon that had a rather short span of life and died a natural death, it is not new to Western philosophy. It had its roots in the ancient tradition of the Greeks. There it appeared in a milder form in the thought of some of the leading philosophers. For example, Aristotle's *araetic,* or virtue-based, ethics appears to be what eventually led to emotivism. It was pointed out in Chapter 2 that Aristotle was prepared to recognize the importance of virtues as the foundation of moral life. Yet he was not willing to formulate any moral laws or principles on the basis of such concrete virtues. It is generally believed that this reluctance on Aristotle's part to recognize moral laws or principles was the result of his rejection of the Platonic forms. This may be partly true. But the more important reason for his reluctance to formulate moral principles is his epistemology, which allowed for incorruptibility in the spheres of science and logic, not in morals. As such, there cannot be any natural tendency in human beings, such as the universal craving for happiness, that could serve as a criterion for morals.[1] Utilitarianism is thereby rejected. Neither did he uphold the Platonic deontology that required that "apart from these many goods there is another which is self-subsistent and causes the goodness of all these as well."[2] He recognized the utility of individual goods, but his logic, physics, and metaphysics, all of which were permeated with a notion of the "ungenerated and imperishable," prevented him from conceiving of moral principles derived from the observation of "many goods." Aristotle was thus left with the conception of individual goods or virtues. He did not condemn them as mere matters of emotion or expressions of opinion. In this respect he differs from the emotivists of the modern period. He only shied away from formulating any moral principles. The celestial or the incorruptible or the imperishable was part of the conception of the physical, not of the moral.

The fact-value problem thus appears to be related to another philosophical issue, namely, the status accorded to psychology in philosophical discourse. Psychology was certainly not a seriously cultivated discipline during the pre-Buddhist period. In the Western tradition Aristotle was considered to be the greatest psychologist. However, in his grand scheme psychology occupies the same status as ethics and aesthetics. More recently, the great deontologist of the Western world, Immanuel Kant, considered psychology a bane to philosophy. The one who came close to solving the fact-value distinction in modern times was Charles Sanders Peirce. Even though he would initiate the pragmatic movement in America, the dent he made in the Anglo-European philosophical tradition was rather insignificant primarily because of his entry into philosophy through the Kantian door. It was left to William James, the psychologist, to break away completely from the Anglo-European tradition and enthrone pragmatism based on radical empiricism as a viable alternative to intellectualism and sensationalism, rationalism and empiricism, transcendentalism and essentialism, and so on.

I have already presented a detailed comparative study of Buddhist and Jamesean psychology.[3] The present discussion therefore will be confined to the manner in which Buddhist psychology provides an interesting solution to this problem of fact-value distinction. This analysis would also apply to Jamesean psychology.

The solution offered by the Brahmanical tradition after it created the dichotomy between fact and value, between *ātma* and *brahma,* is their fusion into one nondual *(advaya)* reality. The Buddha was well conversant with the philosophical problems associated with this fusion. Without expending his energies in solving a problem that need not have been created in the first instance, the Buddha presented his epistemological discoveries in a way that did not generate such a sharp dichotomy.

The previous chapter, dealing with the Buddha's theory of knowledge, highlighted the importance he placed on sense experience. There are many reasons for this detailed analysis of sense experience, the first of its kind in the history of philosophy or psychology. One of them is the avoidance of the fact-value distinction. The oft-quoted passage, which has been separated into three parts and numbered for the purpose of discussion, reads

1. Depending upon the visual sense and the visible object, O brethren, arises visual consciousness; the coming together of these three is contact; depending upon contact arises feeling.
2. What one feels one perceives; what one perceives one reasons about. What one reasons about, one is obsessed with.
3. Due to such obsessions, a person is assailed by obsessed perceptions and concepts in regard to visible objects cognizable by the visual sense, belonging to the past, the future and the present.[4]

Starting from part three of the passage it seems that the Buddha was clearly aware that under normal circumstances sense experience ends with the generation of obsessions. These obsessions are the results of rationalizations about the objects cognizable by the senses and which belong to the past, the present, and the future. In other words, it is not the cognition itself that leads to the obsessions but reasoning about them.

The important question is, Why should reasoning result in obsessions? The answer to this question lies in the manner in which the Buddha, the linguist, formulated his description of the process of perception (in parts one and two) before the rationalizations take over. Part one, explaining the process up to the occurrence of feeling *(vedanā)*, is couched in a language that is passive, the mode of description most appropriate for formulating the principle of dependence. In part two, after the description of feeling, the language takes on the active voice: "What one feels, one perceives; what one perceives, one reasons about." The grammatical change from the passive to the active voice in part two is indicative of a subtle change taking place in the process. Feeling thus serves as a watershed between the natural process of perception and the one colored by the conception of an ego. "I think, therefore, I am" *(mantā asmi)*, the thought that the Buddha advised his disciples to renounce,[5] occurs at this point. This does not mean that feeling is either necessarily associated with such a conception or that it is inherently unsatisfactory or evil. On the contrary, it can occur without such a conception. It is specifically stated that there is satisfaction *(assāda)* in feeling, its evil consequences *(ādīnava)* being its impermanence and change; therefore, freedom from feeling *(vedanāya nissaraṇaṃ)* does not mean its elimination, but rather the abandoning of excessive desire and lust *(chandarāga)* for it.[6] It is this egoless feeling that appears in its noblest and supreme form in compassion. I shall return to this later.

It would be appropriate to ask the question as to what the character of feeling is once it is dissociated from the conception of an ego. Is it just a lifeless lump of experience functioning according to the principle of dependence? The examination of the factors prior to the occurrence of feeling would seem to indicate that this is not so. Feeling is dependent upon contact *(phassa)*. In the essentialist interpretation, contact is bare touch. This cannot be the case because contact is the coming together *(saṅgati)* of three factors: the sense organ, the object of sense, and most important, consciousness *(viññāṇa)*. Because consciousness is the most complex among these three factors and functions in the wake of memory *(sati)*, it seems more appropriate to take contact in the sense of familiarity. In fact, consciousness is sometimes referred to as the "stream of consciousness" *(viññāṇasota)*.[7] When contact is understood in this more comprehensive sense, the stage that follows, represented by part two and beginning with feeling, will inherit that same comprehensiveness. Even though not determined by a conception of an ego, feeling will be determined by whatever else is associated with the three initial factors mentioned in part one. The order in which these three factors (the sense organ, the sense object, and consciousness) are mentioned is also of great significance.

A realist, who believes in the incorruptibility of the object, the corruptibility of the sense organ, and the unreliability of consciousness, would be compelled to say that the object impinges on the sense organ, thereby giving priority to the object. The idealist, on the contrary, will argue that consciousness forms an idea of the object through the instrumentality of the sense organ, and that there is no more to the object than that idea. The Buddha avoided both extremes by emphasizing the importance of both the sense organ and the object in conditioning consciousness, but gave priority to the sense organ. In doing so he abandoned the incorruptibility of the object.

Consciousness itself does not represent a tabula rasa. This excludes the possibility of a direct impression of an object unmediated by any horizon. When the stream of consciousness is stirred up by its dependence on the sense organ and the object, and when the object appears on a horizon, consciousness can be stretched to its limits. This is avoided only by a process of selecting and choosing, which consciousness resorts to at this point. This latter takes place in terms of interest *(saṅkhāra).* Such simple interest determines the very character of consciousness *(saṅkhārapaccayā viññāṇaṃ).*[8] This is why consciousness and interest functioning together are referred to as "becoming" *(bhava),*[9] and together they provide for a conception of an empirical self compared to the metaphysical conception of self or the belief in an ego that emerges with feeling.

I have already argued that enlightenment and freedom do not represent the elimination of the process of sense experience. If, according to the passage analyzed above, sense perception leads to obsession, could there be a way in which that process of perception is transformed instead of being eliminated? This indeed is what is suggested by some of the terms used to define freedom, terms such as *papañca vūpasama* (appeasement of obsessions),[10] *nippapañca* (absence of obsessions)[11] and *saṅkhāra upasama* (appeasement of dispositions).[12] Such appeasement is the result of the total renunciation of the metaphysical conception of a permanent and eternal self, a concept that comes to play at the time when feeling occurs. While the passage quoted earlier explains the process of perception of an unenlightened person, the sense experience of an enlightened person can be described without making changes in the language, as is reflected in the passage. Thus, the entire process could be presented in the language of dependence, retaining all the factors—sense organ, sense object, consciousness, contact, feeling, perception, and reflection—except obsession.

The utilization of the language of dependence to describe the processes of perception and reflection would mean that neither a percept nor a concept, the latter being the means by which reflection is carried out, can be considered incorruptible. The intellectual life of a human consists of substituting a conceptual order (order being accounted for by the process of dependence) for the perceptual order in which experience takes place. As such, there is no reason for the conceptual order to be assigned a privileged status. The nature of the percepts and concepts, as well as the substitution of the latter for the former, is clearly expressed by the very terms used in the Buddhist texts for perception and conception. Perception is represented by the term *saññā* (Skt. *saṃjñā*), which literally means "putting together and knowing." Conception is referred to as *saṅkhā* (Skt. *saṃkhyā*), meaning "putting together and speaking." If they are things "put together," any attempt to discover essences in them would be futile.

With the above definitions of perception and conception, the determination of the truth or falsity of a percept, the meaningfulness or meaninglessness of a concept, shifts from the traditional criterion of essence to that of function or consequence. Within the framework of such a pragmatic definition there cannot be a place for a rigid fact-value distinction. Thus, the revolutionary attempt to accommodate empirical psychology in philosophical discourse by the Buddha in the sixth century B.C. and by William James in modern Western philosophy provided a totally different foundation for moral philosophy.

The Buddha took further steps to eliminate this strict dichotomy. He utilized only one term, *dhamma,* to refer to both fact and value. Interestingly, both singular and plural forms of the term *dhamma,* namely, *dhammo* and *dhammā,* are used in the sense of fact as well as value, the singular and the plural representing two different applications. First, the plural form *dhammā* often expresses the idea of dependently arisen phenomena *(paṭiccasamuppanne dhamme).*[13] As mentioned above, the Buddha, who adopted an enlightened form of pragmatism in the definition of truth, did not allow his thoughts to be influenced by a sharp dichotomy between the physical and the psychological. Hence *dhammā* as dependently arisen phenomena included both the physical and psychological *facts*. Psychological facts were as important as the physical facts that the materialist or the physicalist emphasized. Second, the principle derived from the observation of the functioning of these facts, that is, dependent arising, is then referred to in the singular as *dhammo.*[14] Third, *dhammā* in the plural refer to the virtues *(sīla)* a person cultivates as he or she progresses toward the final goal of freedom while living in the world of dependently arisen phenomena. As such, these virtues, themselves being dependently arisen, function in the context of the factual world exerting their influence on that world even though their cultivation is generally associated with the human. Attribution of moral judgments to animals was done in the later literature, such as the *Jātakas,* and is not found in the earlier canonical literature. Finally, the functioning of virtues is then described in the singular as *dhammo,* this being the moral principle that, like the principle of dependent arising, is neither absolute nor incorruptible.[15]

The elimination of the absolutist fact-value distinction is thus achieved in two different ways. First, by desolidifying the concept of the object through a detailed epistemological analysis, and second, through the renunciation of the belief in absolute laws on the basis of a similar epistemological inquiry.

This does not mean that facts and values are identical or that they should be fused together. What the Buddha presented was a description of facts and values where facts, since they could not be divorced from human knowledge and understanding, are partly subjective, and that values, because they affect the facts themselves, are objective in a pragmatic sense. The abandoning of absolutist and essentialist conceptions of truth enabled the Buddha to take a fresh look at both facts and values.

Is-Ought Problem

The elimination of the extreme version of the fact-value distinction helps to resolve a related issue, namely the is-ought problem. As pointed out in Chapter 1, the Brahmanical tradition utilized an absolute conception of the ought in order to promote its social philosophy based upon the caste system. The materialist thinkers of the ascetic tradition probably rejected the concept even though there is no mention of it in the scanty references to their philosophical thinking. Their denial of the validity of moral discourse and the resultant rejection of the efficacy of human effort did not leave any room for a conception of the ought.

It is well known that the nonsubstantialist Buddha denied any form of absolute existence *(atthitā)*. When the *is* gets defused, so does the *ought*. This is what happened in the Buddha's moral philosophy. When the absolute *is* was replaced with a conception of empirical existence whose meaningfulness is based not merely on sensible cognitivity but also on the actual verifiable *(ehipassika)* consequences, the conception of *ought* also gets de-absolutized and pegged on to that empirical existence. The ought is therefore not an absolute command or necessity, but a pragmatic call to recognize the empirical existence and adopt solutions to whatever problems are associated with it. The Buddha's *Discourse to Kaccāyana (Kaccāyanagotta-sutta)*[16] contains precisely this message.

The discourse is famous for its formulation of the philosophical middle path between the two extremes of absolute existence *(atthitā)* and nihilistic nonexistence *(n' atthitā)*. After rejecting the two extremes the Buddha speaks about the arising *(samudaya)* and ceasing *(nirodha)* of the world *(loka)*. The inability to recognize these two characteristics of the world leads to the two views of absolute existence and nihilistic nonexistence. Thus, the major premise of the Buddha's philosophy of existence, which is also empirical, is arising and ceasing, that is, impermanence *(anicca)*. No major philosopher of the world, Eastern or Western, except probably Heraclitus, has emphasized the idea of impermanence without falling back on some conception of permanence, as did the Buddha. I have already explained how the interpreters of Buddhism misunderstood some statements of the Buddha and attributed to him a theory of permanence (see Chapter 2). The Buddha's assessment of the nature of the factual world then led him to his second major premise about existence, namely, unsatisfactoriness or suffering. This is presented in the statement that follows: a person who is not "bound by approach, grasping and inclination" *(upāyupādānābhinivesa)* characteristic of the ordinary world does not cling to or adhere to the view: "This is myself," this being a reference to the belief in self *(atta)*, subjective as well as objective, held in the Upaniṣadic tradition. Instead, such a person thinks: "suffering that is subject to arising, arises; suffering that is subject to ceasing, ceases." It may be remarked that the Buddha's statement above takes care of two issues at the same time. First is that one should not view the world as possessing permanence. Second is that unsatisfactoriness or suffering is not an essence, something expressed by, say, a rigid designator like pain,[17] but an experience that is variable, subject to arising and ceasing and conditioned by various factors, hence itself impermanent. Thus, we have two of the most important premises in Buddhism presented against the absolutist and essentialist thinking: First major premise; All this (i.e., empirical existence) is impermanent. Second major premise; All this (i.e., empirical existence) is unsatisfactory or suffering.

Time and again the Buddha questioned his disciples or his interlocutors as to whether the second premise (which would normally be considered a value judgment) is derivable from or is entailed by the first premise (which would generally be seen as a statement of fact). The response, even from his most vehement opponents believing in permanence, was always positive.

Once the status of unsatisfactoriness as a fact is established, the Buddha made it the first noble truth. With the recognition of unsatisfactoriness as a fact of the empirical world, the Buddha's perspective enabled him to admit two more related facts, namely, the causality of suffering and the possiblility of its cessation. These then are the second and third noble truths. If unsatisfactoriness is caused, and if there is a possibility of ending it, then comes an obligation to end it. This is the function of the fourth noble truth, namely, the way *(magga)* to end unsatisfactoriness or suffering. The four truths thus demonstrate a method by which an *is* statement can legitimately provide a foundation for an *ought* statement where neither the *is* nor the *ought* are absolute.

CHAPTER 4

The World and the Will

THE FACT-VALUE distinction examined in Chapter 3 also relates itself to another important issue in moral philosophy, namely, the problem of the will, hence the need for the treatment of this subject in a separate chapter. Two of the greatest German philosophers of the modern world, Immanuel Kant and Arthur Schopenhauer, seem to have influenced the philosophical thinking about the notion of the will more than anyone else in the modern world. At a time when philosophers fascinated by scientific developments had begun to raise questions about the validity of ethics and religion as philosophical disciplines, Kant, in his *Foundations of the Metaphysics of Morals,* attempted to resurrect moral philosophy by conceiving of a completely autonomous will. His metaphysics of morals is identical in every aspect with that of the Brahmanical tradition, especially of the *Bhagavadgītā,* with the exception that his categorical imperative is ultimately pegged onto humanity rather than divinity. Schopenhauer, probably the first among modern Western philosophers to undertake a serious study of Indian philosophy, was also one who gave the will an important place in his metaphysics. His proposed concept of the will was the same as the Upaniṣadic notion of self, the inner controller, and with its "great extension" comprehended everything in the world. He even quoted the famous Upaniṣadic formula *tat tvam asi* ("that thou art"). While in the *Upaniṣads* the self is goal-directed in that eventually it is supposed to unite with the moral Absolute, the will for Schopenhauer was a nonrational force, a blind, striving power that functions without ultimate purpose or design. As such it continues to generate conflict and tension. This explains Schopenhauer's extremely pessimistic world view. It seems that he was reworking two concepts, one Upaniṣadic and the other

Buddhist, and putting them together, thereby losing the spirit of both. The Upaniṣadic view is more optimistic in character, whereas Schopenhauer's formulation of that theory partakes of utter pessimism. The Buddhist idea of unsatisfactoriness or suffering was confined to all dispositionally conditioned *(saṅkhata)* phenomena, whereas Schopenhauer converted it to a universal phenomenon.[1]

It is possible to surmise that just as much as the Brahmanical notion of self and its deontology contributed to the amoralism of some of the pre-Buddhist ascetics, even so the concepts of the will presented by Kant and Schopenhauer paved the way for the emotivism in ethics in the modern Western world. The Western philosopher who laid the foundation for emotivism was Ludwig Wittgenstein, believed to have been an enthusiastic reader of Schopenhauer's works during his early days. The most important statement of Wittgenstein on the concept of the will and its relation to ethics is from the *Tractatus,* which reads as follows:

> 6.423 It is impossible to speak about the will in so far as it is the subject of ethical attributes.
>
> And the will as a phenomenon is of interest only to psychology.
>
> 6.43 If the good or bad exercise of the will does alter the world, it can alter only the limits of the world, not the facts—not what can be expressed by means of language.
>
> In short the effect must be that it becomes an altogether different world. It must, so to speak, wax and wane as a whole.
>
> The world of the happy man is a different one from that of the unhappy man.

Since this statement as well as his "A Lecture on Ethics,"[2] moral philosophy had a long, drawn out struggle to achieve some form of recognition and respectability.

The Buddha, faced with a similar situation with the Brahmanical deontology and the amoralism of some of the ascetics, stood on a middle ground between the two extremes. His denial of the Brahmanical notion of an autonomous self also compelled him to reject any notion of an autonomous will. The rejection of autonomy did not compel him to embrace accidentalism *(adhiccasamuppāda).*[3] His conception of dependent arising was the middle ground between absolute autonomy and accidentalism. Dependent arising, as explained in the Chapter 3, is not confined to the physical or what the scientific world considers to be the factual. It includes human initiatives, effort, and so on, as well as human dispositions or tendencies that have been gradually cultivated and developed. Human psychology thus becomes an inalienable part of philosophy if the latter is to have any relevance to human life. For the Buddha, as it was for many other classical philosophers, both Eastern and Western, philosophy involved knowledge and insight *(ñāṇadassana)* into the nature of phenomena *(dhammā),* the most advanced of which is human life.

Even though a completely autonomous will was not something that the Buddha was able to verify on the basis of his knowledge and insight, he was not prepared to deny that there are certain tendencies in the human through which that person is able to plan and initiate processes that may even go against the observed flow of events *(paṭisotagāmī).*[4] If this is what is meant by creativity, it is most visible in human beings. Thus, the Buddha was equally vehement in his criticism of the nihilistic philosophers of the ascetic tradition for their denial of the efficacy of human effort.[5]

There is no one single term in the Buddhist texts that could be considered the equivalent of the term *will*. This means that the so-called will is not one single controlling force, but rather a whole group of tendencies. Furthermore, one may discern two slightly different concepts of the will. The first is the immediately felt tendency to act; the other is the gradually developed tendency to act. The former is expressed by a large number of terms. Prominent among them are

adhiṭṭhāna, determination, and so on;
bala, strength, ability (opposite of *dubbala,* debility);
dhorayha, "carrying a yoke," the ability to shoulder a burden;
kāra (always suffixed to *purusa,* man), activity;
padhāna, striving, exertion, and so on;
parakkama, "moving ahead," hence exertion, endeavor, and so on;
thāma, "standing power," stability, strength, and so on;
ussāha, "lifting up," daring, venture, and so on;
vasa, influence, authority, control, and so on;
vāyama, effort, exertion, and so on;
viriya, vigor, energy, effort, and so on.

Often some of these terms are used in clusters, implying thereby that the so-called will is not one single factor but a whole group of tendencies. For example, the three terms often used together are *purisakāra-puri-*

sathāma-purisaparakkama, where the *kāra* implies activity, *thāma* means the strength to maintain that activity, and *parakkama* connotes the idea of going ahead with that activity. These three terms were probably first used by the ascetics, especially the biological determinists discussed in Chapter 1, who denied the efficacy of human effort.

A passage occuring in several contexts highlighting the Buddha's call to put forth effort reads as follows:

> It is appropriate for a person who has gone forth *(pabbajita)* through confidence *(saddhā)* to initiate effort *(viriyaṃ ārabhituṃ)* [saying]: Let the skin, sinews and bones remain; let the flesh and blood dry up. Whatever should be achieved through human strength, human effort, human endeavor, without achieving that let there be no resting of effort.[6]

This is not a call to extreme asceticism. Instead, it is a graphic description of what human determination can be. The attainment of physical and mental well-being *(attha)* of oneself as well as of others is to be constantly pursued with such determination. This effort can be relaxed only after the attainment of the final goal, namely, enlightenment and freedom. At that point the person is said to be one who has lived the higher life *(vusitavā),* done what ought to be done *(katakaraṇīya),* laid aside the burden *(ohitabhāra),* attained true well-being *(anuppattasadattha),* and so on.[7]

The second concept of the will appears in the explanation of the human. Prompted by his interest in demonstrating the absence of a permanent and eternal self, the Buddha analyzed the human personality into five important constituents, generally referred to as *khandha.* They are body *(rūpa),* feeling, perception *(saññā),* disposition *(saṅkhāra),* and consciousness *(viññāṇa).* The dispositions account for the most comprehensive concept of the will.

The Buddha's emphasis on dependence of phenomena and his rejection of any mysterious substance or entity that functions within phenomena as an inner controller compelled him to focus more on the conception of disposition, which literally means "putting together" *(saṃ + √kṛ).* This means that the Buddha had nothing to do with a world will of the sort that Schopenhauer formulated. As Kant believed, the will is primarily a human phenomenon. However, for the Buddha dispositions that constitute the will are not completely autonomous. They, like any other psychological event, are dependently arisen. I will return to this. The dispositions function along with the other constituents of the human personality. Being part of the personality that "puts things together," the dispositions process themselves as well as other constituents. This is expressed by a passage defining dispositions: "Disposition is so-called because it processes material form or body *(rūpa)*, which has already been dispositionally conditioned, into its present state."[8] (This statement is repeated with regard to feeling, perception, disposition, and consciousness.)

According to this passage, the dispositions, while being dependent, also perform a special function of processing the personality, that is, giving form, guiding or directing, setting up goals, and trying to achieve them. As pointed out elsewhere,[9] the most important function of individuating a person belongs to the dispositions. It can function in the most extreme way—for example, in creating an excessively egoistic tendency culminating in the belief in a permanent and eternal self. For this reason the Buddha considered the self no more than a "lump of dispositions" *(saṅkhāra-puñja)*.[10] Thus, ignorance can determine the way human dispositions function *(avijjāpaccayā saṅkhārā)*, either in creating the belief in permanent existence or in denying the value of the human personality and its activities.

Dispositions are of various types, the most popular among them relating to the body *(kāya)*, speech *(vacī)*, and mind *(mano)*.[11] As such, they are associated with the three types of action *(kamma)*—bodily, verbal, and mental. Even though, in the passage quoted earlier, it is stated that the dispositions process the five constituents of the human personality and give them their identity, the *Discourse to Bhūmija (Bhūmija-sutta)*[12] states that bodily, verbal, and mental actions generate *(abhisaṅkharoti)* bodily, verbal, and mental dispositions, respectively. This again underscores the fact that the dispositions are not autonomous. Most students of Buddhism are aware of the popular statement of the Buddha: "Monks, I say that volition is action" *(Cetanā 'haṃ bhikkhave kammaṃ vadāmi)*.[13] The term *cetanā*, which is translated as volition, is derived from the verb *cinteti*, meaning "thinks," hence the Buddha's statement that follows: "Having thought, one performs an action through the body, speech and mind" *(cetayitvā kammaṃ karoti kāyena vācāya manasā)*. In the *Discourse to Bhūmija* we have the term *sancetanā* (instead of *cetanā*), which is analogous to *saṅkhāra,* and it is argued that when a body exists, because of a volition associated with the body *(kāyasañcetana-hetu)* there arise subjective happiness and suffering. This is repeated with regard to speech and mind.

Here we have an interesting psychological explanation: coordinating thought or volition *(sañcetanā)* is the spring of action, and action generates disposition. Together they explain several complicated issues relating to moral philosophy debated in the modern world. For example, on the one hand, there are those who insist that a person is responsible for any voluntary or conscious action. They are the upholders of free will. On the other hand, there are those who argue that a person could not have acted differently because of that person's upbringing, background, or the society. They are the determinists who deny free will. The *Discourse to Bhūmija* represents the Buddhist solution to this dilemma, and it works as follows. Volition is the most important factor in determining whether a person is responsible or not for an action. If an action is accompanied by volition, a person is held responsible; if not, that person is not held responsible. However, there could be a situation where a person might act with no volition immediately evident but could still be held responsible. The dispositions come to play at this point. While volition may be an immediate act of deciding, dispositions represent the gradually built up character involved in decision making. According to the *Discourse to Bhūmija,* such character building can be conditioned by ignorance on the part of oneself or by the presence of another person, that is, by a role model. It can take place knowingly *(sampajāna)* or unknowingly *(asampajāna).*

The second type of disposition referred to in the discourses is what may be described in Freudian terms as "life instinct," or the will to live *(āyu-saṅkhāra).* The references are mostly to the life of the Buddha. In the *Discourse on the Great Decease (Mahāparinibbāna-suttanta),* which is a connected account of the last days of the Buddha, it is said that he was once afflicted with a severe illness and experienced pangs of death *(maraṇantikā vedanā).* However, he bore the pain with mindfulness and awareness, thinking: "It is not proper for me to attain the final release *(parinibbāna)* without addressing the lay disciples and without greeting the Community of monks and nuns. Let me control this illness with effort and remain [for a while] by determining the disposition to live *(āyu-*

saṅkhāra)."[14] At the end of three months, at a place called Capala cetiya, he is said to have abandoned or released the disposition to live. He traveled a little longer, probably a few weeks, and passed away at Kusinārā.

The above concept of disposition then leads to the view that grasping after life or maintaining the will to live can eventually generate rebirth. The entire *Discourse on the Arising of Dispositions (Saṅkhāruppatti-sutta)*[15] is devoted to an explanation of this view. According to the discourse, a person who has attained enlightenment and freedom is not reborn anywhere.

Third, there is a less-known group of three dispositions: disposition for merit *(puññābhisaṅkhāra),* disposition for demerit *(apuññābhisaṅkhāra),* and disposition for permanence *(āneñjābhisaṅkhāra).*[16] However, it is not stated that those who cultivate these dispositions obtain the things they are disposed to achieving. Instead their consciousness gets colored by them.

Even though the Buddha did not recognize a will in the world, he did recognize the impact of the human dispositions, or the so-called will, not only on the human personality, but also on the world at large. Our physical surroundings, our amenities of life—housing, clothing, utensils—and in a major way our towns and cities, art and architecture, culture and civilization—and, in the modern world, even outer space—come to be dominated by human dispositions. Karl Popper calls it the World Three.[17] For this very reason, the Buddha, describing the grandeur of a universal monarch, his palaces, elaborate pleasure gardens, and other physical comforts, referred to all of them as dispositions.[18]

CHAPTER 5

Individual and Society

THERE IS NO denying that the concept of a person's identity gets entangled with any conception of society. The concept of identity in its strong sense is expressed in the Pali language by the phrase *so . . . so* (he . . . he). Thus, we have the statement: *so attā so loko,* "he is the self, he is the world". Here the individual self and the world are identified by the use of the term "he" *(so).* The phrase "he is the self" expresses the most important character of that entity, namely, agency. That identity is established when it is claimed that "he, I will be after leaving here" (a literal translation of *so pecca bhavissāmi*), and it is further strengthened by the assertion that "I, the permanent, enduring, eternal, not subject to change, will remain as such being eternal" *(nicco dhuvo sassato aviparināmadhammo sassatisamaṃ tath' eva ṭhassāmi).*[1]

It is not necessary to spend too much time trying to prove that this is the theory of self and world in the early *Upaniṣads* until the conception of *brahma* gained prominence as the nondual moral Absolute. The concepts of *ātma* and *brahma* in the early *Upaniṣads* are indicative of the directions in which speculation proceeded. The concept of *ātma* emerged as a result of an essentialist pursuit, that is, the search for an essence or substance in each individual person. The notion of *brahma* is the culmination of the quest for the ultimate social reality.

The Buddha, psychologist par excellence, observed that these two pursuits had psychological origins, especially human anxiety *(paritassanā).*[2] Yet, after his rejection of these views on epistemological grounds, their proponents were beginning to claim that these truths were the result of nonsensuous yogic intuitions.[3] A refutation of this latter epistemological claim is not easy. The Buddha was not unaware of this difficulty. He realized that the other party could always argue that the person who rejects such a claim has not reached the highest stage of concentration and therefore has failed to develop the intuition required for the verification of such a reality or realities. Rebuttal of this argument is not possible. All that can be done is to state one's epistemological position, indicate what sort of claim about reality can be made in terms of that standpoint, and leave the opponent with his own theory *(vacāvatthu)*. This is precisely what the Buddha did during his confrontation with the metaphysician Jānussoṇi regarding the question about "everything" *(sabba)* as recorded in the *Discourse on Everything (Sabba-sutta)*, which I highlighted in previous writings.[4]

The Buddha was also aware that these ideas, though psychological in origin, become more and more fossilized as they are continually reflected upon, expressed, discussed, and debated. In this process they also become embedded in the means of communication, namely, language. As a result, the problems become highly complicated. Whatever language a social group utilizes eventually ends up being a mirror of reality for that particular group. The more sophistication the language attains, the search for essences and universals becomes more and more entrenched therein. Thus, in the Indian context, the fluidity of linguistic expression, as was evident in the Vedic language, was gradually eliminated as special sciences intended to preserve the *Vedas* (i.e., the *vedāṅgas*) emerged. Two of them, etymology *(nirukti)*, devoted to the study of the ultimate constituents of language, and grammar *(vyākaraṇa)*, the science of meaning or relationship among those ultimate constituents, are not unrelated to the concepts of the individual and society as they appeared in philosophical speculations in the Upaniṣadic period. The culmination of etymological studies with the compilation of Yāska's *Nirukta* and the consummation of grammatical studies in Pāṇini's *Aṣṭādhyāyī* produced the Sanskrit ("well done") language. The loss of the fluidity of the language thus gave further impetus to the original philosophical search for essences and universals.

For this very reason, when the Buddha wanted to enunciate a middle path that avoided conflicts, a purely epistemological analysis was not sufficient. It had to go hand in hand with an analysis of language in which the ideas had become fossilized. He found that the two extremes of *ātma* and *brahma* were already linguistically grounded with the recognition of the two disciplines, etymology and grammar, respectively.

At least five terms are used in the early discourses to refer to language. They are used singly or in clusters. The terms are *nirutti* (etymology), *sāmañña* (universal), *vohāra* (usage), *sammuti* (convention) and *paññatti* (conception).[5] Among these, the first two reflect the philosophical pursuits during the Buddha's day. The last three represent the Buddha's own understanding and conception of language. For him, etymological studies may not be useless as long as they are not directed at discovering essences. Even so, the study of universals or relations would be useful as long as it was not intended to discover incorruptible universals, as was the case in Platonism. In fact, at a later date the great Indian grammarian, Bhartṛhari, did utilize the study of grammar to establish the one incorruptible ultimate, *brahma*. Thus, when the Buddha wanted to express his middle path in morals that would avoid conflicts *(raṇa)*, he resorted to an analysis of language. On this occasion he utilized the two terms *nirutti* and *sāmañña* to refer to language, and then advised his disciples not to grasp *(abhinivesa)* on to it (i.e., language as etymology, *nirutti*) and not to overstretch *(atisāra, atidhāvana)* it (i.e., language as universals, *sāmañña*).[6] The defossilizing of the concepts of the particular and the universal in language, an undertaking pursued with great enthusiasm and success by the Buddhist logician, Dignāga, at a later date, contributed to a new perspective relating to the individual and society.

The recognition that language evolved gradually and that it continues to change depending upon various factors—physical, psychological, social, and cultural—with no ultimates is implied in the three other terms, *vohāra*, *sammuti*, and *paññatti*, used by the Buddha to refer to language.

The *Discourse on the Origins (Aggaññā-suttanta)*[7] is a demonstration, through a skillful analysis of language, of the meaninglessness of the Brahmanical caste system as a foundation for society and morals. According to the discourse, the belief that "the brahman class is superior, others are inferior; brahmans alone are purified, not non-brahmans, brahmans are the sons of *brahma*, born of its mouth, created by *brahma*, inheritors of *brahma*," arises because of the nonrecollection of the past *(porāṇa)*. Sarcasm is involved in the statement that it is possible to perceive how a brahman woman comes to season, conceives, gives birth to, and nurses a baby. Then it proceeds to evaluate the four castes in terms of virtues and vices.

However, simply stating this was not sufficient. The very concepts involved in language, including the concepts of the castes, had to be analyzed. At this point, the discourse takes up the past and analyzes it, going back to speculative beginnings, for the actual origin of things is said to be "inconceivable" *(anamatagga)*.[8] This fanciful account of the evolution of the world process after a period of dissolution describes the gradual emergence of life on earth, the evolution of human life, society, customs, economics, and politics, as well as morals. It goes hand in hand with the explanation of the possible evolution of language starting with the basic element, namely, the word (*akkhara*, considered to be incorrigible, *akṣara*, by the Brahmanical tradition). It assumes that the very first occurrence of a word is arbitrary, a result of an exclamation or a sudden outburst with no known meaning.[9] (One such term, almost universal in its occurrence, whether it be in the inflexional languages of the Indo-European family or in the monosyllabic Mongoloid languages, is the term for mother, which is no more than one derived from the cry of a baby as it makes its entry into this world.)

If this were to be the possible origin of most words and terms, once they are continually used, they become part and parcel of the language as usage. In addition, there are words or terms, still accidental in origin and not the result of exclamations or sudden outbursts but conscious attempts to agree on some understanding and expressing it. These can be comprehended under language as convention. Language is also the means by which a person expresses his or her experience of objects, events, relations, and so on, physical or psychological. This cognitive aspect of language is highlighted when language is referred to as "expression," "indicator," or conception. What this means is that even if the actual origin of a term may be clouded in mystery, once a term is adopted, its signification evolves or changes depending upon the physical, psychological, and social conditions. There is no absoluteness with regard to the meaning or the use of language, an idea that is now being floated around by some of the leading philosophers of the modern world as "language drift."[10]

The above analysis of language enabled the Buddha to present concepts of individual and society without creating a sharp dichotomy where the reconcilation became almost impossible. Thus, the individual is neither a totally independent entity with absolute inalienable rights nor one that is totally determined by the society with no claim to any rights. Similarly, society is neither a mere conglomeration of individuals without any relations nor an absolute reality imposing its authority on the individual without restrictions. Avoiding both these extremes, the Buddha adopted a middle path of explanation.

Two interesting dialogues, one from the *Upaniṣads*[11] and the other from the Buddha's discourses,[12] could provide an interesting starting point in the discussion of the individual. The first is a conversation between Yajñavalkya and Maitreyī and the second between King Pasenadi of Kosala and his queen, Mallikā. The relevant part of the *Upaniṣads,* which is an extensive dialogue, and the Buddhist discourse, which is very brief, are quoted below.

> Then Maitreyī said: "What should I do with that through which [that is, the whole world filled with wealth] I may not be immortal? What you know, Sir,—that indeed, tell me!"
>
> Then Yajñavalkya said: "Ah, Lo, dear *(priya)* as you are to us, dear is what you say! Come, sit down. I will explain to you. But while I am expounding, do you seek to ponder thereon."
>
> Then he said: "Lo, verily, not for love of husband is a husband dear, but for the love of the Soul *(Ātman)* a husband dear.
>
> Lo, verily, not for the love of the wife is a wife dear, but for the love of the Soul a wife is dear.
>
> Lo, verily, not for the love of sons are sons dear, but for the love of the Soul sons are dear.
>
> Lo, verily, not for the love of wealth is wealth dear, but for the love of the Soul wealth is dear.
>
> Lo, verily, not for love of Brahmanhood is Brahmanhood dear, but for the love of the Soul Brahmanhood is dear.
>
> Lo, verily, not for the love of Kshatrahood is Kshatrahood dear, but for the love of the Soul Kshatrahood is dear.
>
> Lo, verily, not for the love of the worlds are worlds dear, but for the love of the Soul worlds are dear.
>
> Lo, verily, not for the love of the gods are the gods dear, but for the love of the Soul the gods are dear.

> Lo, verily, not for the love of beings are being dear, but for the love of the Soul beings are dear.
>
> Lo, verily, not for the love of all is all dear, but for the love of the Soul all is dear."

The Buddhist dialogue reads:

> In Sāvatthi . . .
>
> At that time King Pasenadi of Kosala was with his queen, Mallikā, on the terrace of their palace.
>
> Thereupon the King Pasenadi questioned Queen Mallikā thus: "Mallikā, is there anything which is dearer *(piyatara)* than the self *(attanā)*?"
>
> "O, Great King, I do not have anything dearer than the self."
>
> "For me too, Mallikā, there is nothing dearer than the self."
>
> [The king, having visited the Buddha reported this conversation to him.]
>
> Thereupon the Buddha on that occasion, having understood the meaning, uttered this verse:
>
> "Having surveyed all directions with the mind, you did not discover anything dearer than the self. Similarly, the individual self is dear to others. Therefore, one who is desirous of oneself should not hurt others."

The two dialogues seem very similar. The theme is the same; the conclusion is also the same. However, there is an enormous difference between the metaphysical backgrounds. I have already explained at length the implications of the Upaniṣadic concept of self. The Buddha's disagreements with that concept have also been noted. What is important, therefore, is to find out how one can speak of oneself without stretching it out to imply a permanent and eternal self and how that concept of the individual self can be utilized to inculcate proper social behavior, that is, nonviolence. For the psychologist Buddha, it is one thing to say one loves oneself, and it is yet another to assume that that self is a mysterious and permanent agency lying behind the psychophysical personality.

In discussing the concept of the will, I have already explained the role of dispositions in individuating a person. Dispositions in their most subtle form represent "interest," while in their gross form they constitute craving, greed, and so on. The healthy life between self-deprivation and self-indulgence comes from calming or appeasing dispositions *(saṅkhārasa-*

matha) and adopting a restrained concept of self. Thus, psychologically, one who is "desirous of self" *(attakāma)* is one who does not totally abdicate self-interest. The person may be prepared to renounce all worldly things; still, that person need not destroy him- or herself. It is only in this comparative sense that the self is considered to be dear. Thus, the Buddha did not advocate total self-sacrifice as it was done in the deontological systems founded on theism.

Self-interest, even in its most rudimentary form, is not accommodated in the theistic systems. This is because, until after conception, an individual is not responsible for his or her coming into existence. The parents are the projenitors, not the creators of life. Therefore, even though the parents may carry some responsibility, in the ultimate analysis a person owes his or her existence to the Supreme Being, or God (*īśvara, brahma,* and so on). As a result, the ultimate stage of the moral life cannot accommodate human self-interest; it has to be totally renounced. The Buddha adopted the Brahmanical conception of *brahma* only after a great deal of revision. First he rejected the idea that it is a creator God.[13] Second, he refused to accept it as the ultimate moral Absolute that determined the caste system and its duties. However, he retained the moral content of *brahma* by depicting it as a moral deity, Brahmā, who is capable of merely providing protection to those who tread the moral path but does not or cannot control their decisions to follow the path or not, let alone be their creator. As pointed out in Chapter 11, the vacuum created by the nonadmission of a creator God in the explanation of the moral life, especially moral obligation, was filled by the concept of karma and rebirth. With the recognition of the possibility of rebirth, the Buddha was admitting that the individual as well as the parents were responsible for that individual's coming to be. As such, self-interest of both parties are involved. Self-interest, in its most rudimentary form, is a commonplace psychological fact. It need not be identified with compounded interest such as greed and deceit, as was done by Glaucon in the Platonic dialogues. That identification has dominated much of Western philosophy up to modern times.[14]

This being the case, the Buddha's conception of society hinges on the self-interest *(saṅkhāra)* of both oneself and others. "Love thy neighbour not for any reason but because that person has the same self-interest as thine." Thus, it is this extremely significant human interest that makes a society meaningful. Society is not a mere aggregate of individuals or something superimposed on the individuals from above, but mutual self-interest. Yet this self-interest is not another self-subsistent entity or essence in the individual, but one that depends on the physical conditions, or the environment, upon the historical and cultural background, upon the hopes and aspirations of the individuals. The analysis of the human into the five factors of the psychophysical personality *(pañ-cakkhandha)* was intended to account for such an individual.

Setting up of absolute limits *(mariyādā)* with regard to the definition of the individual[15] or the society[16] was not looked upon as an enlightened activity. Individual welfare as well as the welfare of all beings can be achieved by those whose thoughts are not entangled in such limits *(vimariyādikatena cetasā)*[17] and who cultivate thoughts of boundlessness *(appamañña)*.[18] The cultivation of the four higher states *(brahmavihāra)*, namely, friendliness *(mettā)*, compassion *(karuṇā)*, sympathetic joy *(muditā)*, and equanimity *(upekkhā)*, will be facilitated only by such conceptions of the individual and society.

PART TWO

THE MORAL LIFE, THE PRINCIPLE, AND JUSTIFICATION

CHAPTER 6

The Noble Life *(Brahmacariya)*

DURING THE BUDDHA'S day the two terms used to describe the moral life were *brahma* and *dharma*. Whatever their original meanings were,[1] as mentioned in Chapter 1, the terms had come to imply a "moral Absolute" and a "[caste-] duty," respectively. However, the Buddha avoided both meanings and utilized them to refer to the moral life in general. The Buddha's rejection of the Upaniṣadic use of the term *brahma*, implying a moral Absolute with which union is sought, is found in the *Discourse to the Great Steward (Mahāgovinda-suttanta)*. Herein, referring to one of his previous lives when he was a brahman named Mahā-Govinda and instructed his disciples on the way to achieve union with the Brahma world *(brahmalokasahavyatā)*, the Buddha maintained that this noble life did not lead to freedom.[2] Note that the term *brahma* is never used in itself except when referring to a class of divinities. It is always used with the suffix *cariya* 'practice', 'behavior', and so on, or *yāna* 'the way', 'the vehicle', and so on, or *vihāra* 'living', 'state', and so on. Therefore, the term *brahmacariya* is more appropriately understood as the "noble life." This was the Buddha's way of avoiding the metaphysics of the Upaniṣadic use. However, since the term *dhamma* was not used in the *Upaniṣads* to refer to the moral Absolute, the Buddha seems to have adopted this term, even without the suffixes mentioned, to refer to the morals as well as the moral principle.

The noble way of life *(brahmayāna)*, or the way of morals *(dhammayāna)*, is said to be the incomparable victory in the war *(anuttarasaṅgāmavijaya)* against evil.[3] It is generally divided into three parts: the beginning *(ādi)*, the middle *(majjha)*, and the conclusion *(pariyosāna)*, all parts being considered good *(kalyāṇa).* Ānanda, the constant companion of the Buddha and one who did not attain enlightenment and freedom as long as the Buddha lived because of his attachment to the Buddha, was generally inclined toward transcendentalism.[4] As such, he perceived only one-half *(upaḍḍha)* of the noble life to be good.[5] In doing so, he made the very same distinction between the religious life and the moral life that the transcendentalists resorted to throughout the history of philosophy and religion. For most of them the highest stage of moral perfection, which they would include under the religious, is totally incompatible with what is considered to be the moral life. There has to be an absolute break between the moral life of ordinary human beings and the highest state of enlightenment and freedom, that is, *nirvāṇa.* The transcendentalists understood the phrase "above the world" *(lokuttara)* as being "beyond the world." They went by the principle that what is distinguishable is also separable, which is a purely essentialist principle. We have already pointed out that the Buddha avoided setting up absolute limits *(mariyādā)* (see Chapter 5). Identity and difference, in their absolute forms, were rejected by the Buddha. For him, there is a thread of continuity in the conception of human life, the world, and the highest state of moral perfection a human can achieve. It is somewhat similar to the early Chinese conceptions expressed by the three characters *jen* or human (人), *ta,* the great, the earth (大), and *t'ien,* or heaven (天). These three ideograms express the continuity within three distinguishable concepts without splitting them into totally different entities. Concepts are not absolute and incorruptible entities but devices, that is, something put together *(saṅkhā)* for the sake of expressing an experience that is itself similarly put together (see Chapter 3), hence possessing fringes or horizons that relate them. The noble life, its beginning, and the end, are thus connected, hence the Buddha's admonition that the noble life in its entirety *(sakalaṃ),* not merely one-half *(upaḍḍhaṃ),* is good.[6] It is said to be good in the beginning *(ādikalyāṇa),* good in the middle *(majjhe kalyāṇa),* and good at the end *(pariyosānakalyāṇa).*[7] It is a stream, or a continuity, of a human who goes against the normal temptations characteristic of the uncultivated and immoral character. As the unwholesome and harmful tendencies are gradually overcome and the human personality is gradually transformed, the very conceptual apparatus utilized in describing that person needs to be changed without doing violence to the continuity. Kicking the ladder after climbing to the top of the roof is a purely transcendentalist way. This issue will be discussed in Chapter 10.

The Buddha refers to the higher life adopted by the six heterodox teachers (see Chapter 1) as being unsatisfactory.[8] He also mentions the four types of the so-called noble life he followed during the six futile years before his enlightenment. They consisted of the practice of ultimate austerity *(paramatapas)*, ultimate wretchedness *(paramalūkha)*, ultimate disgust *(paramajeguccha)*, and ultimate solitude *(paramapavivitta)*.[9] In addition, he speaks of the "noble life of a young person" *(komārabrahmacariya)* prevalent during his day. It consisted of being proficient in the *Vedas* and adopting the moral life recommended in the Brahmanical tradition, such as the nonviolation of the caste system.[10] He does not characterize it as unsatisfactory, but maintained that it has limitations *(mariyādā)*.

Reportedly, according to the Buddha, enthusiasm *(āsā)* alone is not sufficient for someone to achieve the fruits of the noble life. The most important factor in the realization of the goal of the noble life is the understanding of the "genesis" *(yoni)* of things.[11] Conditionality *(idappaccayatā)* and dependent arising represent the Buddha's explanation of the genesis, or arising, of things. Therefore, the noble life he advocated is one that should be directed at eliminating any perspective contrary to dependent arising. This includes the ideas of self-causation, external causation, both, or noncausation.[12] Neither the belief in a permanent and eternal self as the agent of activity within oneself, nor the belief in an external reality or power, nor a combination of these two views, nor the assumption of accidentalism can help a person to achieve freedom from suffering. Thus, the various versions of the noble life presented in the discourses describe alternative means of eliminating wrong views *(micchādiṭṭhi)* and developing a right perspective *(sammādiṭṭhi)*.

The wrong views mentioned earlier are not easily overcome. They are the results of attachment or aversion. The development of right views is also not easily achieved by an ordinary person. Both call for a long period of training. However, in laying out this path of training the Buddha wanted to begin by describing the nature of the life of ultimate purity or the goal of the noble life so that the trainee, even though starting with the cultivation of simple virtues of social relevance, would not lose track of that ultimate goal.

A life of complete renunciation *(pabbajjā)*, which culminates in enlightenment and freedom, is therefore defined as one that is wholly fulfilled *(ekantaparipuṇṇa)*, wholly pure *(ekantaparisuddha)*, and polished like a conch shell *(saṅkhalikhita)*, compared with the life of a householder, which is confined *(sambādha)* and dusty *(rajopatha)*.[13] Such a description of renunciation was a further incentive to those who would want to remain in the household and undertake the practice of morals that called for an element of renunciation.

Several differing versions of the noble life are presented in the discourses. The first[14] consists of the following:

1. Cultivation of virtues *(sīla)*
2. Restraint of the senses *(indriyasaṃvara)*
3. Elimination of the five mental obstructions *(nīvaraṇa):* covetousness *(abhijjhā)*, ill will *(vyāpāda)*, sloth and torpor *(thīna-middha)*, restlessness and worry *(uddhacca-kukkucca)*, and excessive doubt *(vicikicchā)*
4. Development of the four preliminary stages of contemplations *(jhāna)*
5. Development of the threefold higher knowledge

The second[15] version contains the first four items of the above list, but instead of the fifth stage, which involved the development of insight, the second version returns to the restraint of the senses, giving a different description of it. Instead of saying that upon seeing an object one should not grasp onto a substance and characteristics, it recommends that the perceiver not become enamored with the pleasant object and disgusted with the unpleasant one. This is said to lead to freedom.

The third and most important version of the noble life is the eightfold path.[16] Since virtues are considered the springboard for the practice of the eightfold path, it is possible to assume that steps two, three, and four of the above list can be replaced by the eightfold path. In fact, whatever is to be achieved through the cultivation of these steps is also achievable through the more comprehensive eightfold path. The noble eightfold path is also the last of a list of practices, such as the four states of mindfulness *(satipaṭṭhāna)*, the four comprehensive strivings *(sammappadhāna)*, the four psychic powers *(iddhipāda)*, the five faculties *(indriya)*, the five powers *(bala)*, and the seven factors of enlightenment *(sattabojjhaṅga)*. The practice of each one of these is said to serve the long-lasting establishment of the noble life, the well-being and happiness of many, and so on.[17]

The following detailed analysis of the noble life will therefore be made in terms of the three parts: the beginning, which constitutes the virtues, the middle, which is comprehensively covered under the eightfold path, and the conclusion, which is freedom.

CHAPTER 7

Virtues
The Beginning of the Way

THE *Discourse on Brahma's Net (Brahmajāla-suttanta)*[1] presents the most comprehensive description of virtues *(sīla)* in the early discourses. The content of the discourse was considered so significant that the Buddha, questioned by Ānanda, provided a string of titles for it, indicating the manner in which he wanted it to be understood. The titles are as follows:

1. "Net of meaning or welfare" *(atthajāla)*
2. "Net of morality" *(dhammajāla)*
3. "Net of Brahma" *(brahmajāla)*
4. "Net of views" *(diṭṭhijāla)*
5. "Incomparable victory in war" *(anuttara saṅgāmavijaya)*[2]

The discourse consists of two parts, the first containing a detailed description of the virtues and the second involving an equally detailed analysis of sixty-two forms of metaphysical views, most of which are now identified as theories that were actually held by the pre-Buddhist thinkers.[3] For modern scholarship, this discourse provides two separate sources, one for the study of virtues and the other for information about pre-Buddhist views *(diṭṭhi)*, with no philosophical unity between the two. For most scholars, the "net of Brahma" meant the metaphysical views of pre-Buddhist India; it had nothing to do with the conceptions of welfare and morality of the first part of the discourse. However, taken as a whole the two parts provide an extremely sophisticated thesis on morals.

If we consider the order in which the material is presented in the discourse, it would be possible to see a very consistent and coherent argument followed throughout the discourse. It starts with the story of a wandering ascetic named Suppiya who, along with his disciple, Brahmadatta, was traveling along the road connecting Rajāgaha and Nālandā. At the same time the Buddha, with about five hundred of his disciples, was traveling the same stretch of road. Reportedly Suppiya disparaged the Buddha, his teachings, and his disciples, while Brahmadatta praised them. When the monks reported this to the Buddha, his admonition to them was that they should neither be depressed and displeased at any such disparagement nor be gladdened and elated by any such praise, for both responses would be harmful. Instead they were asked to carefully examine such criticisms and praise. This was then made the occasion for explaining the virtues *(sīla)* in terms with which an ordinary person would speak well of the Buddha. An ordinary person could evaluate the Buddha in terms of these virtues representing the visible behavior of a person, for the Buddha's moral attainments are beyond their comprehension.

Since this discourse was meant to be a major presentation of the Buddha's conception of morality, a simple exposition of the virtues would not have sufficed. As explained in Chapter 1, pre-Buddhist thinkers had either moved toward absolutism in ethics, as did those of the Brahmanical tradition with its theory of *brahma,* or advocated a total rejection of moral discourse, as did the materialists. The reasons for this were their metaphysical views regarding the nature of ultimate reality. It was therefore necessary for the Buddha to examine all these different metaphysical ideas that served as foundations of the moral theories different from his own.

In this connection it is important to note how the Buddha tried to present the Brahmanical conception of the moral Absolute, *brahma,* in his own terms. In the discourses we hear of the world of Brahmā as the highest among the worlds of gods and humans. These gods are not celestial in the often-understood sense of the word. They are not permanent and eternal abodes of existence. The gods have reached this states as a result of their virtuous deeds as humans; they are reaping the consequences of their karma. They are neither creators nor representations of the Almighty. In the early discourses there are two Brahmās that appear rather prominently. First is Brahmā Sahampati, who often functioned as a protector of the virtuous. He is said to have appeared before the Buddha and pleaded with him to preach the doctrine at the time when the Buddha, immediately after his enlightenment, was hesitant to preach what he had discovered, fearing he would not be understood. At Brahmā's request the Buddha decided to speak of his enlightenment. The second is Baka Brahmā, one who was in search of the permament, the eternal, and the immutable who, according to the Buddha, was on a "mission impossible" *(alabbhanīya ṭhāna)*.[4] (Interestingly, *baka* is a term for a heron or a crane, symbolizing a hypocrite, a cheat, or a rogue, for it is regarded as a bird of great cunning and deceit as well as circumspection.) In a sense, the two Brahmās represent the contents of the discourse. Taken as a whole, the discourse is a clear exposition of the "net" *(jāla)*, that is, the web of metaphysical beliefs that can accompany any discourse on human welfare *(attha)* and morality *(dhamma)*. It is also a "victory in the war" *(saṅgāmavijaya)* against metaphysical speculations, which the pre-Buddhist thinkers tried to justify either on the basis of an inappropriate appeal to yogic intuition *(ātappaṃ anvāya padhānaṃ anvāya anuyogaṃ anvāya sammāmanasikāraṃ anvāya)* or on the basis of reason *(takkapariyāhataṃ vīmaṃsānucaritaṃ)*. It is indeed a total rejection of the Aristotelian view that there can be invariable laws, such as those assumed in science and logic, and that ethics deal with the variable virtues.

It is also interesting to note that the Buddha considered his understanding of the metaphysical theories to be profound.[5] Anyone who would praise him for such understanding would be extending a genuine form *(yathabhuccaṃ)* of praise compared with that of the ordinary person who depended merely *(mattakaṃ)* upon limited *(appa)*, this worldly *(ora)* virtues *(sīla)*.[6] These remarks are significant for several reasons. Virtues are important as the nuclei of the moral life. They are the stepping stones of the moral life.[7] "Having established oneself in the virtues, a sagacious one proceeds to develop thought *(citta)* and wisdom *(paññā)*."[8] As such, virtues are not sufficient in themselves. On the one hand, to be virtuous is not the ultimate goal of life, and on the other, there is no one virtue that may be considered the ultimate or the essential one. "Be virtuous *(sīlavā)* but not made of virtues *(sīlamaya)*" was the Buddha's admonition.[9] It was a clarion call to avoid any deontological coloring of the virtues or the moral life. If there is to be any ultimate goal, it is freedom.

Once the overall meaning of the *Discourse on Brahma's Net* is understood, it is possible to engage in a detailed analysis of the virtues. The discourse lists virtues under three categories: minor *(cūḷa),* middling *(majjhima),* and major *(mahā).* This gradation is not based on the general significance of the virtues, but on the status of the persons who cultivate them. Thus, the so-called minor virtues, both negative and positive, are recommended for all, while the middling and major ones, even though of lesser significance in terms of gravity, are for the ascetics and brahmans who live on the faith-inspired sustenance *(saddhādeyya)* provided by the laypeople. In other words, even minor offenses by those who have committed themselves to a moral life are amplified.

The minor virtues include the ten precepts discussed throughout the discourses. Among these, the first seven involve not merely the abstentions, that is, what is generally considered evil, the avoidance of which enables a person to build up his or her moral character, but also the more positive aspects that represent a moral person's impact on the world or the social nature of the virtuous life. These seven virtues, therefore, are embodiments of the ultimate criteria of the good, namely, the welfare of oneself *(attahita)* and the welfare of others *(parahita).* These criteria will be discussed at length later. The seven virtues are as follows:

1. Refraining from taking life *(pāṇātipāta),* abandoning severe punishment *(daṇḍa)* and arms *(sattha),* being modest *(lajjī)* and loving *(dayāpanna),* extending friendliness and compassion to all living beings *(sabbabhūtahitānukampī)*
2. Refraining from stealing *(adinnādāna),* accepting what is given *(dinna),* hoping for the given, living with a self that has become pure *(sucibhūta)*
3. Abandoning a lower life *(abrahmacariya),* leading a higher life *(brahmacariya),* being remote (from evil, *ārācārī*) and detached from vulgate sensuality *(methunā gāmadhammā)*
4. Refraining from confusing speech *(musāvāda);* speaking the truth *(saccavāda);* being realistic *(theta),* trustworthy *(paccayika),* and nonconflicting with the world *(avisaṃvādako lokassa)*
5. Refraining from malicious speech *(pisuṇavāca),* (i.e., not creating dissentions among people), being one who unites those that are divided *(bhinnānaṃ sandhātā),* promoting those who are united *(sahitānaṃ anuppadātā),* delighting in harmony *(samaggārāmā),* delighted in harmony *(samagaratā),* enjoying harmony *(samagganandī),* and speaking harmonizing words *(samaggakaraṇiṃ vācaṃ bhāsitā)*

6. Renouncing harsh speech *(pharusavācā);* resorting to speech that is blameless *(neḷā),* pleasing to the ear *(kaṇṇasukhā),* lovable *(pemanīyā),* appealing to the heart *(hadayaṅgamā),* urbane *(porī),* and attractive *(manāpā)* and pleasing *(kantā)* to the multitude *(bahujana)*
7. Abandoning frivolous talk *(samphappalāpa);* speaking at the appropriate time *(kālavādī);* speaking what has come to be *(bhūtavādī;* speaking the truth), what contributes to welfare *(attha),* to morality *(dhamma),* to discipline *(vinaya);* making statements that are referential *(nidānavatī),* timely *(kāla),* with horizon *(pariyantavatī),* and fruitful *(atthasaṃhita)*

These are the basic virtues repeatedly emphasized in the discourses. In addition, there are at least four different types of virtues mentioned. They are those of the forest *(araññaka),*[10] of the household *(gehasita),*[11] attractive to humans *(manussakanta),*[12] and attractive to the worthy ones *(ariyakanta).*[13] The first refers to the behavior of animals in their forest habitat. For the behaviorist this would be the most natural, if there were to be anything called natural virtues. In comparison, human virtues may appear artificial. This may be true only in regard to situations where humans moralize purely in terms of selfish motives. The Buddha did not opt for any such hedonic calculus. Utilizing the parable of the elephant caught in the wild and trained by a mahout, the Buddha argued that human beings can train themselves in the virtues attractive to humans by abandoning the virtues of the forest.[14] In placing human virtues over and above that of the forest the Buddha recognized the importance of human rationality, an undeniable asset of the human species.

The second and third virtues constitute one category, namely, the worldly morals *(lokiya dhamma).* The first of these refer specifically to the virtues of the household, the obligations of the members of a family. The second is broader in scope. They are virtues attractive to the members of the human family. While human rationality is what distinguishes forest virtues from those of the humans, rationality alone is not what determines the virtues of the human family. Rationality along with welfare serve as criteria for the determination of the virtues of the human world. It is this human welfare that makes these virtues meaningful and obligatory.

The fourth virtue represents the virtues of the noble person, the worthy one *(ariya)*. It adds another dimension to human virtues by providing a further criterion for their justification, which is freedom. The question as to what this freedom is has been debated since its first formulation. The nature of that freedom and how the virtues contribute to the realization of that freedom will be discussed in Chapter 9. For the present it may be stated that the virtues, according to the Buddha, gradually lead to the attainment of that ultimate goal.[15]

While virtues serve as a springboard for ultimate freedom, they are not without immediate benefits. A person possessed of a noble body of virtues *(ariya sīlakkhandha)* is said to enjoy unblemished subjective happiness.[16] Such a person does not experience fear *(uttāsa)* and trepidation *(chambhitatta)* in this life and has no fear of death in a future life *(samparāyika maraṇabhaya)*.[17] Even the negatively stated virtues such as refraining from taking life are said to provide freedom from fear *(abhaya)*, from hatred *(avera)*, and from injury *(avyāpajjha)* to countless beings, with the practitioner him- or herself enjoying the same benefits. Hence, these are called the supreme charities *(mahādāna)*.[18] One of the more important questions that may be raised at this point is, Would it not be possible for a person who practices the virtues of noninjury, and so on, to be subjected to injury, and so on, by others who are nonvirtuous? The Buddha's answer is that a virtuous person is not remorseful, or does not regret his own behavior. Lack of remorse or regret *(avippaṭisāra)* is one of the most significant fruits *(attha)* or benefits *(ānisaṃsa)* of wholesome virtues *(kusalāni sīlāni)*.[19] The Buddha then proceeds to enumerate a series of further consequences of the absence of remorse or regret. These, in order, are delight *(pāmujja)*, joy *(pīti)*, happiness *(sukha)*, concentration *(samādhi)*, knowledge and insight into what has come to be *(yathābhūtañāṇadassana)*, disenchantment and absence of lust *(nibbidā-virāga)*, and finally knowledge and insight into freedom *(vimuttiñāṇadassana)*.[20] This psychological and intellectual transformation is said to be natural *(dhammatā)*. The naturalness is emphasized when it is said that a virtuous person need not make an effort *(na cetanāya karaṇīyaṃ)* to be nonremorseful or nonregretful.

There is no denying that the above psychological and intellectual transformation of a virtuous person is on the whole a subjective achievement. The Buddha did admit this. He spoke of four types of persons.

1. One who is devoted to one's own welfare *(attahita)* and cultivates the five virtues but is not devoted to the welfare of others *(na parahita)* and therefore does not cause others to cultivate the virtues
2. One who is not devoted to one's own welfare *(na attahita)* and therefore does not cultivate the virtues but is devoted to the welfare of others *(parahita)*, causing them to cultivate the virtues
3. One who is devoted neither to one's own welfare nor to that of others *(neva attahita na parahita)*, hence neither cultivates the virtues himself/herself nor causes others to cultivate the virtues
4. One who is devoted to one's own welfare and cultivates the virtues, while at the same time is devoted to the welfare of others by causing others to cultivate the virtues[21]

Needless to say, the last is the best. Indeed, in another discourse, the Buddha describes a noble person as one who is virtuous *(sappurisa)*, that is, one who cultivates the virtues, and then proceeds to define one who is nobler *(sappurisena sappurisatara)* as one who cultivates the virtues and causes others to do so.[22] Since this is the highest ideal, clearly stated in the early discourses, it would be inappropriate to demean that ideal as one of selfishness and of "low disposition" *(hinādhimukti)*, as it came to be described by some of the later Buddhists.[23] The social character of this ideal was clearly emphasized by the Buddha when he maintained that the scent of the virtuous person wafts in every direction, even against the wind *(paṭivāta)*.[24] Such a person need not necessarily be an enlightened one. Even a virtuous layperson *(upāsaka)* falls into the category of one who works for the welfare of both oneself and others.[25]

CHAPTER 8

The Eightfold Path
The Middle of the Way

I MENTIONED in previous discussions of virtues that they serve as a springboard for the practice of what is properly called the moral life. In the early discourses, this moral life is generally represented by the "noble eightfold path" *(ariya aṭṭhaṅgika magga)*.

Like the term *vaṇṇa* (Skt. *varṇa*), used to refer to the caste system even though it originally meant "color" (and the origin of the caste system actually can be traced to differences in the skin color of the invaders and the aboriginies of India), the term *ariya* (Skt. *ārya*) was originally used to refer to the invading race, the Āryans. In the Buddhist texts the term is used in a moral sense and does not carry any racial implications. It is often translated into English as "noble." The criterion of nobility is therefore not race, color, or social status, but the achievement of safety, security or peace *(khema)*, well-being *(sovatthika, su-atthi-ka, svastika)*, and joy associated with such peace and well-being.[1] Peace, well-being, and happiness thus characterize the path as well as the ultimate goal *(agga)*, that is, freedom, to which it leads. Thus, the way of life and its goal that the Buddha pursued before enlightenment are referred to as "ignoble quest" *(anariya pariyesana)* compared to the path and the goal he discovered after enlightenment, which are designated the "noble quest" *(ariya pariyesana)*.[2]

The eight constituents of the path *(maggaṅga)* are right view *(sammādiṭṭhi)*, right conception *(sammāsaṅkappa)*, right speech *(sammāvācā)*, right action *(sammākammanta)*, right livelihood *(sammāājiva)*, right effort *(sammāvāyama)*, right mindfulness *(sammāsati)*, and right concentration *(sammāsamādhi)*.

Two important characteristics of the eightfold path are that it is the middle of the moral life as well as a middle way. Virtues, mentioned above, are the stepping stones to a serious undertaking of the moral life. Freedom is the climax or the conclusion. The eightfold path is thus the middle part of the noble life. However, it is better known as the middle way *(majjhimā paṭipadā)* between two extremes *(anta):* a life of indulgence in the pleasures of sense *(kāmasukhallikānuyoga)* and indulgence in self-mortification *(attakilamathānuyoga).*[3] A life of indulgence is rejected more for social reasons. It is low, vulgar, and individualist. It is motivated by possessive individualism. A life of self-mortification is avoided mostly for psychological reasons. It is not characterized as low, vulgar, and individualist; it is simply painful. Both, however, are ignoble and unfruitful. This would mean that the path avoiding these extremes should be both noble and fruitful. Fruitfulness, or *pragma,* is not the only criterion in deciding what is good. The Buddha was certainly aware that usefulness could be interpreted in a rather selfish way. By adding nobility as a characteristic of the way, he was giving it a moral tone. This is the function of the term *sammā* (right), used to qualify all the eight constituents.

Epistemologically the term *sammā* carries the sense of comprehensiveness, which implies avoidance of shortcuts in deciding what is right and wrong, on the one hand, and renunciation of any attempt to account for everything, on the other, the latter being impossible in the absence of omniscience. Comprehensiveness involves examining every possible senario and recognizing whatever is relevant. In most cases, the irrelevant appears to be metaphysical issues that cannot be resolved by an appeal to both radical empiricism and inductive reasoning (see Chapter 2). It is therefore necessary, when analyzing each constituent of the path, for us to keep in mind that the term "right" means precisely this nonabsolutist and moderate character.

The emphasis that the Buddha laid on epistemology is again reflected in his formulation of the path. Thus, right view heads *(pubbaṅgamā)* the list of eight constituents.[4] Right view, as I pointed out elsewhere,[5] should not reflect the absolutist true-false dichotomy. Right view is the middle standpoint between a dogmatic view *(diṭṭhi),* which is true in an ultimate sense, and no view *(adiṭṭhi),* that is, not adopting a view or taking any standpoint. Right view then would be the most comprehensive view that can be adopted within the limitations of human knowledge and understanding.

An interesting discussion of the noble eightfold path is found in the *Discourse on the Great Forty (Mahācattārīsaka-sutta)*.[6] It consists of two versions of the first six constituents of the path. Thus, right view is twofold. The first is the view still associated with defilements *(sāsava)*, leaning toward (accumulation of) merit *(puññabhāgiya)*, and resulting in the establishment of rebecoming, or rebirth *(upadhivepakka)*. This is the view that asserts the fruits of the religious life consisting of charity, offering, sacrifice, and actions well done and ill done, which recognizes this world, a world beyond, mother, father, beings of spontaneous birth, as well as ascetics and brahmans who have gained insight into the nature of the world, all of which were denied by the amoralist Ajita Kesakambali. Even though this view is considered a right view in opposition with the wrong view held by Ajita, it is still associated with defilements. This is because while it enables a person to be virtuous, there is yet craving for merit and grasping after becoming *(bhava)*.

The second view is also a right view but improves upon the first in adopting views such as the four noble truths,[7] thereby strengthening wisdom, the faculty of wisdom, and the power of wisdom. This view is of one whose mind is free from defilements *(anāsavacitta)* and is therefore called "the constituent of the path that is above the ordinary world" *(lokuttaramaggaṅga)*.[8]

Opposed to the wrong conceptions, which are dominated by thoughts of sensual pleasures *(kāma)*, ill will *(vyāpāda)*, and injury *(vihiṃsā)*, the right conceptions are thoughts dominated by renunciation, absence of ill will, and noninjury. These are no doubt virtues. Most people, including ordinary human beings, would recognize their value. However, there is yet another form of right conception that ordinary human beings would not be able to comprehend, that is, verbal disposition *(vacīsaṅkhāra)*, which are an argument *(takka)*, a reflection *(vitakka)*, a conception *(saṅkappa)*, a complete focusing *(appanāvyappanā)*, and an application of mind *(cetaso abhinīhāro)*. This is a reference to one of the most complicated issues relating to the philosophy of conception and language, hence beyond the comprehension of the ordinary virtuous person. A name or a term in a language representing a concept is generally taken to correspond to a thing or an entity. Even some of the most sophisticated philosophers, not to mention ordinary persons, have taken this correspondence to be absolute. The opposite view, sponsored mostly by transcendentalist thinkers, assumes that there is no relationship whatsoever between the two and that reality is ineffable. Here the Buddha, discussing right conception, is warning that one has to be careful in dealing with concepts for they involve verbal dispositions. As such, they are neither incorruptible nor meaningless. This is the foundation of the middle path adopted in regard to language as expressed in the *Discourse on the Analysis of Peace (Araṇavibhaṅga-sutta)*[9] and elaborated upon in some of the later treatises such as the *Kathāvatthu* and the *Vajracchedikā-prajñāpāramitā.*

Right view and right conception were not part of the virtues discussed in Chapter 7. The seven virtues discussed there are now comprehended under the next three constituents of the path. Right speech is not as complicated as the right view and right conception. Remember that refraining *(veramaṇī)* from the four vices—confusing speech, malicious speech, harsh speech, and frivolous talk—constituted the virtues of speech. The distinction made in the discourse between worldly right view and the right view that is above the world is that, in the case of the latter, this means complete abstinence, expressed by the use of three more terms—*ārati, virati,* and *paṭivirati.* Such abstinence applies to right action and right livelihood as well.

We have already observed that virtues are the stepping-stones of the moral life and that they are not valued for their own sake. The Buddha wanted to recognize their usefulness and then proceed to explain something more useful, namely, the moral life. The definition in the previous paragraph of the first six constituents of the path represents an extremely sophisticated method of harmonizing virtues *(sīla)* and morals *(dhamma* or *adhisīla).*

It may also be noted that the remaining three constituents of the path were not included under the category of virtues. The discourse reiterates the idea that each one of the four constituents—right conception, right speech, right action, and right livelihood—revolves around right view, right effort, and right mindfulness.

Elsewhere,[10] right effort is defined as the decision, exertion, effort, and determination of mind to the nongeneration of evil and unwholesome tendencies, to the elimination of such tendencies that are already arisen, to the production of wholesome tendencies that are not yet arisen, and to the maintenance of those that are arisen.

Right mindfulness represents the reflection *(anupassanā)* relating to the body *(kāya)*, feeling *(vedanā)*, thought, and ideas (*dhammā*, i.e., ideas pertaining to the experienced phenomena). Such reflections enable a person to overcome covetousness and discontent.[11]

Right concentration consists of the attainment of the four preliminary stages of contemplation, which culminate in the development of unprejudiced perception or equanimity with regard to what is perceived (*upekkhā*, lit., "taking a close look"). It is also considered a middle standpoint *(tattramajjhattatā)* in the way in which we perceive ourselves and the world.

The eightfold path does not include the four higher stages of contemplation, which are meditative techniques directed at gradually eliminating the perceptual and conceptual worlds. Such contemplations were looked upon by the Buddha as means of temporarily resting the ever-inquisitive mind from struggling with the objects of experience, hence a temporary state of peace and calm. It is after emerging from such a state that the Buddha is said to have realized the nonsubstantiality of phenomena. However, the eightfold path is supposed to culminate in knowledge, and that means taking an altogether different route.

According to the above information gleaned from the early discourses, the noble eightfold path is the moral life that serves as a bridge between the life of virtues and ultimate freedom. Thus, we have the concept of the higher virtues.[12] The gradualness of the path thus consists in starting with the basic virtues relating to a life of social harmony and moving on to the more comprehensive moral life. A sharp dichotomy between the virtues and the moral path is avoided by including the sevenfold virtues in the moral path as four of its constituents. The inclusion of right view and right conception in the moral path and the prominence given to them serve as an answer to the moral skeptic's question, Why virtue? More important is the definition of these two as having two aspects, as shown in the diagram.

The first aspect answers the question, Why virtue? by providing a basic epistemological foundation for the virtues, or the beginning of the way. The second aspect, which is a more sophisticated or higher analysis

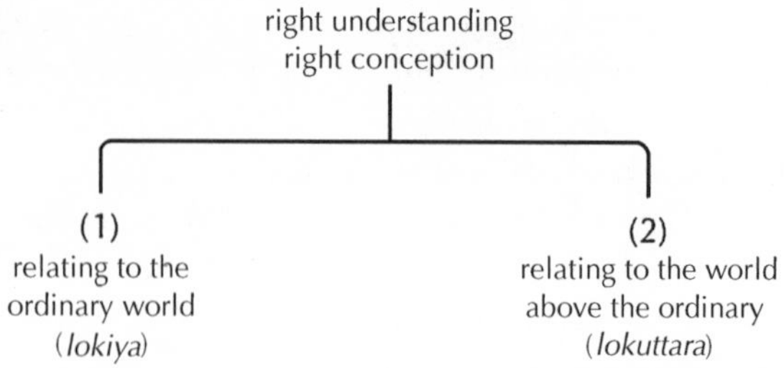

(sāmukkaṃsikā dhammadesanā), includes the enlightened one's description of the nature of existence (i.e., the four truths) as well as the nature of that description itself (namely, conception and language). It is an epistemological justification of the conclusion of the way, that is, freedom to which the path is supposed to lead. A typically Buddhist meaning of the constituents of the path is highlighted when they are said to deal with what has come to be *(yathābhūta).* Thus, right view is the view of things as they have come to be *(yathābhūtassa diṭṭhi),* right conception is conception of things as they have come to be *(yathābhūtassa saṅkappa),* and so on.[13] Right view and right conception thus play an extremely important role in placing the moral life between the ordinary world of virtues and the ultimate goal of the noble life, namely, freedom and peace.

It is indeed the ultimate goal, which is not a constituent of the moral path, that serves as an incentive to follow the path. It serves the function of an imperative. This is the point at which right exertion and right mindfulness play their roles. With no absolute moral law to guarantee results, the one who traverses the moral path has to put forth effort constantly, and, with no absolute knowledge or omniscience (i.e., the ability to predict the future with certainty), the wayfarer needs to be constantly vigilant and mindful.

With such moral rectitude and strength of character, the wayfarer could focus on the final step of the path, namely, right concentration. And the four preliminary stages of contemplation indeed open the door to higher knowledge *(abhiññā).*

The idea that the moral path does not conform to any incorruptible law is clearly expressed in a passage repeated in two discourses.[14] Among those phenomena that are dispositionally conditioned *(saṅkhata dhamma),* the noble eightfold path is said to be the supreme. This statement reflects the sentiments of those who often argue that morals are made for humans; humans are not made for morals. In other words, the path needs to be modified depending not only upon the physical, emotional, and intellectual status of the wayfarer as he or she progresses along, but also according to the situations and contexts he or she faces in this world of constant becoming and change. This does not mean the path has no uniformity and is a purely haphazard one. The uniformity of the path is determined by its ultimate goal because there is no variety in it. Freedom, which may be described by means of a variety epithets (see Chapter 10), is the dispositionally unconditioned *(asaṅkhata).* This means that ultimate freedom is not something that can be adjusted to one's own interest. The idea is expressly stated in a discourse in the *Aṅguttara-nikāya.*[15] It is said that, just as the great ocean is filled with a variety of gems, even so the "doctrine and discipline" *(dhammavinaya)* is filled with a variety of gems such as the four states of mindfulness, the four states of exertion, the four bases of psychic power, the five faculties, the five powers, the seven factors of enlightenment, and the noble eightfold path. These represent a great variety in the modes of practice. However, just as the great ocean has only one taste, namely, the taste of salt *(loṇarasa),* so does the "doctrine and discipline" possess one taste, namely, the taste of freedom *(vimuttirasa).*

The above description of the path may leave the wrong impression that once a person attains enlightenment and freedom the path can be completely ignored and left behind, that there is no need for that person to be moral anymore. However, this is not the impression one gets from the discourses, for the Buddha is twice described as the great sage who continually treads the noble path *(ariye pathe kamamānaṃ mahāmuniṃ).*[16] This problem will be discussed further in Chapter 9.

CHAPTER 9

Freedom
The Conclusion of the Way

EVER SINCE its initial formulation in the very first discourse he delivered to the world, the Buddha's conception of freedom *(nibbāna)* had been the subject of innumerable disquisitions by both classical and modern scholars. There were controversies about the nature of this freedom even during the Buddha's day. The attempt to depict the state of freedom as a nondual Absolute comparable to that of the *Upaniṣads* has continued among both Buddhist and non-Buddhist scholars for nearly 2,500 years. I have favored the tradition that interpreted the conception of freedom as one that is consistent with the Buddha's central doctrines of nonsubstantiality and dependent arising. Freedom in this nonabsolute sense is explained in some detail in my most recent publication.[1] Without recounting that material I shall confine my present analysis to the personal and social relevance of the concept of freedom.

Here too the major traditions are not of much help. While the Theravāda emphasized the personal relevance of freedom, Mahāyāna insisted upon the social relevance. The former assumed that one has to first attain enlightenment and freedom and instruct others. It utilized the statements of the Buddha, such as the one defining an erudite *(paṇḍita)* who is supposed to establish himself or herself in an appropriate situation before instructing others.[2] There was nothing wrong with this idea if not for the fact that those who upheld it postponed helping others until they themselves attained enlightenment and freedom, which was either too slow in coming or, in some cases, did not come at all. A natural reaction to this came from those who believed that the achievement of one's own freedom should be postponed until everyone has been helped across to the shores of freedom. Thus, we are left with two Buddhist concepts, the individualist and socialist, pitted against one another. A sharp dichotomy between the individual and the society, between the concepts of particular and universal, was gradually established. I have already pointed out the inapplicability of such dichotomies in the explanation of the Buddhist doctrine. It is therefore necessary to examine the Buddha's conception of freedom in the light of the moral philosophy embodied in the discourses themselves in order to discover the personal as well as the social relevance of that concept.

The attainment of enlightenment and freedom on the part of the Buddha was a personal experience. The social, moral, and religious background made it not only a personal experience, but also a unique one. For example, the domination of Indian society by the priestly class may have been less than what it was before and after the Buddha. The evidence for this is the emergence of the warrior class into prominence and the consequent admission by the brahmans that it was a superior creation. Yet, the Buddha's criticism of the fourfold caste system in the discourses, second only to his criticism of the Brahmanical conception of self, seems to indicate that the moral life was based upon a wrongly conceived theoretical foundation. Even though in that context some people suffered discrimination and deprivation, it would not be fair to say that the society as a whole was evil and immoral. It would be more appropriate to hold that the moral life was misdirected. The theoretical foundation, as well as the goal of the moral life, was confused and ill conceived. This is why five of the six heterodox teachers rejected the Brahmanical moral theory. In spite of their noncommitment to any moral theory, they probably were people of great moral standing. Jainism, as mentioned earlier, advocated another extreme, self-destructive view.

It is in this background that the Buddha's enlightenment and freedom appeared so unique. For this reason it started as a purely personal experience. However, that personal experience becomes part of the social experience as well, depending upon how that experience is integrated into the moral life he recommended. The nature of his enlightenment has already been explained (see Chapter 2). It served as the new foundation of the moral life. Freedom is the goal or conclusion. This freedom permeates the entire moral life like the singular taste of salt permeates the waters of the oceans. If the Buddha assumed that ultimate freedom is beyond the world, as the transcendentalists did, then the goal is severed from the path and not integrated with the moral life. He avoided such a perspective. For him, ultimate freedom is above the world, like the lotus that rises above the water without being severed from its root in the water.

An absolute break between the moral life and its goal or conclusion (freedom) is avoided by the manner in which the Buddha described them. The conclusion *(pariyosāna)* of each one of the factors of the moral life, that is, of the eightfold path, is the disciplining, or restraining, of passion *(rāga)*, hatred *(dosa)*, and confusion *(moha)*.[3] The conclusion of the entire moral life, or the eightfold path, is the waning or complete cessation *(khaya)* of passion, hatred, and confusion.[4] The disciplining, or restraining, which begins with the practice of the virtues, culminates in the waning or complete cessation of the causes that lead to bondage and suffering. *If the immoral life is one of passion, hatred, and confusion, the moral life has to start with their restraint and conclude with their complete elimination.* The absolute break would then occur not at the point at which the moral life reaches its culmination, but at the time when the immoral life is replaced with a moral life. Compared with that immoral life, the moral life and its conclusion will be above the world.

In the early discourses, one can notice two different conceptions of the world *(loka)*. First is the world available to sense experience, that is, the objective world subject to arising and ceasing, to evolution and dissolution.[5] The second is the world that is engrossed with the concepts of existence and nonexistence.[6] Existence is not simple empirical existence, but permanence *(sassata)*, and nonexistence does not mean change and disappearance, but total annihilation *(uccheda)*. This second conception of the world, especially the belief in permanence, makes the first one appear unreal in spite of the manner in which it impinges on the individual, whether he or she is unenlightened or enlightened, in bondage or in freedom. In fact, as emphasized in Chapter 2, the second conception of the world encourages the belief in a world beyond, a world other than the one experienced here. The Buddha's enlightenment is the result of overcoming this massive intellectual obsession. In keeping with that enlightenment he rejected the two extremes of behavior, namely, indulgence in pleasures of sense and self-sacrifice. Thus, the moral life, whether it is at its beginning, middle, or conclusion, has to be what is conducive to one's own welfare and the welfare of others.

Furthermore, the relationship between the Buddha's conceptions of the way and its goal could not be understood in terms of the popular theories of teleology or instrumentalism. These theories assume that the path is important and relevant only insofar as it leads to the desired goal. Once the goal is reached, the path becomes irrelevant. For the Buddha, the moral life that leads to ultimate freedom, or *nirvāṇa,* does not become irrelevant once freedom is achieved.

There are two ways in which one can look at ultimate freedom. First, the complete elimination of greed, hatred, and confusion is not an easy task. The Buddha was certainly aware that very few would aspire to reach heaven *(sagga),* conceived to be a place where one can enjoy high-quality pleasures of sense.[7] This is because it requires at least the cultivation of the virtues. If that were the case, there would be even fewer people who would aspire to attain ultimate freedom and enjoy the happiness associated with it, for cultivating the morals requires enormous effort and commitment. In this sense, freedom is a personal achievement and experience. If this is all that is involved in the attainment of freedom, the Theravādin is right and the Mahāyānist is wrong.

However, if freedom is to be achieved by following any one of the paths discussed earlier, it can never be a purely personal experience. From the very initial stages of the path, which involves the cultivation of the virtues through the intermediary stage of practicing the eightfold path, and so on, the wayfarer has to be a social animal, not an individualist. Here the Theravādin is wrong and the Mahāyānist is right. The middle path between the so-called Theravāda and Mahāyāna has to be one in which the extremes of individualism and socialism are renounced. That renunciation can come only after a proper understanding of the nature of existence, namely, dependent arising, which is the foundation of the Buddha's conception of freedom. With that understanding, it is not possible for a person to attain freedom without affecting the society, for to follow the virtues and the eightfold path is to affect the society in a radical way.

Furthermore, an enlightened one is not above the *dhamma;* he is one who respects the *dhamma.*[8] As mentioned in Chapter 8, he continues to tread the noble path *(ariye pathe kamamānaṃ).* At one point he is described as a "human being *(manussabhūtaṃ),* perfectly enlightened, one who has tamed himself, is concentrated, traversing the noble path *(iriyamānam brahmapathe)* and deligted in the appeasement of thought."[9] Even the Buddha, who had attained enlightenment and freedom, had to continue to tread the moral path because it is not an absolutely fixed blueprint valid for all time. Neither is freedom a static state, like the Brahmanical moral Absolute; it is one of continuous challenges. This is because even the enlightened one cannot be absolutely certain about everything that would happen in the future, whether it be in the physical, social, economic, or political worlds. One has to adjust one's behavior according to the changes taking place in the world of dependant arising. What remains the same in this world of change, and the only thing that the enlightened one can be certain about, is his/her response to that world, that is, he/she must not allow room for temptations that would lead to rebecoming *(punabbhava)*.[10] This is metaphorically expressed in the discourses with the concept of Māra, which is the embodiment of temptations. The Buddha is said to have attained enlightenment and freedom after defeating the forces of Māra. Yet Māra did not give up. He continued to stalk the disciples as well as the Buddha. Two instances where Māra followed the disciples looking for their rebirth (i.e., trying to find out whether they had fallen pray to temptations) are those relating to Godhika[11] and Vakkhali.[12] These are instances where the individuals had attained freedom at the moment of death, and Māra is said to have been despondent *(dummano)*. However, the Buddha continued to live for at least forty-five years after his attainment of enlightenment and freedom. The stories of Māra stalking the Buddha even after the latter is said to have vanquished the former is a symbolic representation of the idea that temptations themselves are not static, but are dependent on changing conditions and environments. Thus, even the Buddha had to be constantly vigilant *(appamatta)*.

While the Buddha's attainment of enlightenment and freedom was a personal experience and achievement, he did not remain docile for the rest of his life. He worked assiduously for the welfare and happiness of all beings, through compassion for the entire world *(sabbalokānukampako)*.[13] As such, he earned titles such as the person of great compassion *(mahākāruṇiko)*,[14] the physician for the entire world *(sabbalokatikicchako)*,[15] an incomparable surgeon *(sallakatto anuttaro)*[16]—titles that highlight enlightenment and freedom as a social ideal. While the Buddha's own life represented one of exemplary social service, with his way of formulating the moral life and its benefits, there was no need for his disciples to wait until they attained freedom to work for the welfare of others. The basic character of the moral path outlined earlier is that it concerns oneself and others from the very beginning, starting with the cultivation of the virtues, through the practice of the eightfold path, and more so after the attainment of enlightenment and freedom. A glance at the stories of monks and nuns during the Buddha's day, as recorded in the *Thera-therī-gāthās,* clearly indicates the social character of the moral path as well as its conclusion, where one person's achievements inspired another's undertakings. These monks and nuns did not live in isolated huts and did not sit in meditation all the time and gather together only at the time when meals were served. The *ārāma* was a place of "delight," where those who had attained freedom and those who were on their way lived together, helping each other and inspiring still others who were interested in entering the way. While the Buddha was the person to whom both monks and nuns often turned for advice, it is interesting to note that the nuns spoke more of the support and assistance they received from other monks and nuns who had attained enlightenment and freedom.[17] This is in contrast to the monks, who looked to only other monks for assistance. This is understandable considering the social background, where the monks were more self-reliant than the nuns, the latter being subjected to centuries of discrimination. Those who had attained freedom were the role models for others.

CHAPTER 10

The Status of the Moral Principle

AFTER YEARS of study and reflection on the various philosophical theories available during his day, and after leading a life of renunciation for more than six years before his enlightenment and freedom, the Buddha had the confidence to abandon the search for permanence. His realization of the dependent arising of phenomena enabled him to to make a determined effort to overcome passion and hatred, attachment or aversion. Enlightenment and freedom thus became closely linked. That freedom enabled him to reformulate the principles that could replace the belief in absolute laws, whether they be in the explanation of the physical world, human psychology, society, politics, morals, or even language. Reportedly, after his attainment of enlightenment and freedom, the Buddha remained seated under the *bodhi* tree for seven days enjoying the bliss of emancipation *(vimuttisukha)*.[1] At the end of the seven days he began to reflect on the nature of existence. The whole night, immediately following the enjoyment of freedom, was devoted to reflection on the principle of dependence, which was his explanation of existence. These reflections are embodied in three verses:

> When indeed phenomena appear before a brahman as he remains ardent and reflective, all his doubts subside as he realizes their causal nature.
> When indeed phenomena appear before a brahman as he remains ardent and reflective, all his doubts subside as he comes to know the cessation of causes.
> When indeed phenomena appear before a brahman as he remains ardent and reflective, he scatters away the regiment of Māra (temptation) like the sun that illuminates the sky.[2]

The moral path leading to freedom and happiness, outlined above, is based upon the moral content of his experience. Therefore, it is fair to assume that the moral principle is itself based upon that moral experience and its formulation in the form of a path. This is further evident from the Buddha's epistemology, which rejects deductive inference in favor of induction. In this sense, the moral path and its conclusion, which he outlined in the discourses, (as explained in the preceding chapters), should serve as the raw material for the formulation of the moral principle.

The most significant statement of the Buddha regarding the status of the moral principle is introduced in the context in which a monk named Ariṭṭha, a former vulture trapper,[3] is said to have held the view that certain vices that the Buddha claimed to be harmful *(antarāyika)* were actually not so.[4] One example quoted in the discourse is sensual desire *(kāma)*, which the Buddha had declared to be of little satisfaction, leading to a lot of suffering and tribulation, and fraught with peril. Up to ten parables were used to illustrate this unfortunate character of sensual desire. Thus, Ariṭṭha's denial of the evil consequences of sensual desire is a rather strong challenge to anyone who wished to formulate a moral principle on the basis of the validity of virtues. It is possible that Ariṭṭha, like some of the philosophers of the ascetic tradition, was reacting negatively to the absolute moral laws of the Brahmanical tradition. The Buddha made this an occasion to deliver another one of those important discourses, the theme of which has continued to be utilized throughout the history of Buddhism, the most prominent instance being the *Vajracchedikā-prajñāpāramitā*.[5]

The Buddha began his response to Ariṭṭha by indicating how there can be a wrong understanding of the Buddha's ideas embodied in the discourses, verses, expositions, and so on. This is when a person studies a text without testing the meaning *(attha)* through intuitive wisdom and, consequently, utilizes the ideas for the wrong purpose. Employing the parable of the person who grasps a water snake *(alagadda)* by the tail and comes to ruin, and another who grasps it by its neck and does not face such unfortunate consequences, the Buddha advised his disciples to accept his ideas only if they understood them correctly. If they did not understand them, they should make further inquiries either from him or the experienced monks and nuns. Then came the most significant statement of the Buddha.

> I discourse to you, monks, on the doctrine that is comparable to a raft, for the sake of crossing over and not for grasping. . . . By you who know the doctrine to be comparable to a raft, even the goods have to be abandoned let alone the bad ones. (*Kullūpamaṃ vo bhikkhave dhammaṃ desissāmi nittharaṇatthāya no gahaṇatthāya, . . . Kullūpamaṃ vo bhikkhave ājānantehi dhammā pi vo pahātabbā pag eva adhammā.*)[6]

This passage contains two uses of the term *dhamma,* one referring to the *statement* of the doctrine, and the other describing the *content,* namely, good and, bad *(adhamma).* As I mentioned elsewhere,[7] these are related uses. A text or a discourse is a statement about ideas, and this latter, if meaningful, refers to facts about the world of experience. When it is said that the statement of the doctrine (i.e., discourses, and so on) is like a raft, that simile is applicable to the ideas or facts as well. Some of the persistent problems in philosophy have been due to the distinction one tends to make between language and its contents. It is generally assumed that a statement is a weak representation of facts. The ineffability thesis, in whatever form it appeared, has this assumption as its foundation. The Buddha did not contribute to any such thesis.[8] The Buddha's epistemology does not allow room for the recognition of invariable facts on the one hand, and variable descriptions on the other. His nonsubstantialism is so radical that the idea of permanence has no way to escape. Indeed, the language and the texts, as well as the contents, whether the last pertains to facts or values, are like the raft with which a person crosses over a great stretch of water, from a bank that is dangerous and frightening to one that is secure and peaceful, from suffering to happiness. Thus, after applying the metaphor of the raft to the statement of the doctrine, the Buddha proceeded to do the same with regard to its contents.

The remainder of the discourse is devoted to a lengthy refutation of the idea of permanence. He refers to six foundations of views *(diṭṭhiṭṭhāna):* the physical body *(rūpa);* feeling *(vedanā);* perception *(saññā);* dispositions *(saṅkhāra);* what is seen, heard, conceived, cognized, attained, sought for, and reflected upon *(diṭṭha, suta, muta, viññāta, patta, pariyesita, manasā anuvicarita)*(which, of course, seem to include everything conceivable and which are the activities of consciousness, *viññāna*); and the concepts of the world *(loka)* and the self *(atta),* which, it was the hope of the Brahmanical thinkers, would become one and remain permanent and eternal.[9] These are the foundations on which human beings construct their notions of self, a mysterious agent or inner controller or owner of the individual as well as the world. The Buddha agrued that if one does not conceive of a self relating to these subjective as well as objective aspects of experience, one does not generate any anxiety *(paritassanā)*.

The purpose of this lengthy discussion of nonsubstantiality is to dispel doubts the monks and nuns entertained as a result of Ariṭṭha's heresy. It was an attempt to show that one can conceive of a moral principle without having to admit anything permanent and eternal.

The moral principle is another application of the general principle of dependent arising. The scholastics identified at least five such principles *(niyama)* relating to the following:

1. Physical (inorganic) world *(utu)*
2. Physical (organic) world *(bīja)*
3. Sphere of thought or mental life *(citta)*
4. Individual and social behavior *(kamma)*
5. Moral life *(dhamma)*[10]

Even though the scholastics include under the category of the moral principle *(dhamma-niyāma)* only the naturalness associated with the life of the *bodhisattva* as described in the *Discourse on the Great Lineage (Mahāpadāna-suttanta)*,[11] thereby signifying a move toward transcendence, it is possible to argue that the entire noble eightfold path can be comprehended under the *dhammaniyāma*, for it is the complete moral life compared to the virtues discussed in Chapter 7. Specifically, a monk "depending upon the virtues, establishing oneself on virtues, developing the noble eightfold path, thoroughly practicing the noble eightfold path, attains progress, loftiness and fullness with regard to the morals."[12] In other words, the virtues serve as a springboard for the practice of the moral life, this latter consisting of the noble eightfold path. It was pointed out that the noble eightfold path comprehends all three factors required for the attainment of ultimate freedom, namely, virtues *(sīla)*, concentration *(samādhi)*, and wisdom *(paññā)*, hence its more exalted status. For the present we are interested in the path primarily as representing the moral principle.

The moral life, functioning as part of the general principle of dependence *(paṭiccasamuppāda)*, also shares with it every characteristic of that general principle. First, the moral life is objective *(tathatā)*, not a mere fabrication of the human imagination. Its objectivity is vouched for by the good consequences reaped by the person who practices it. It is in this sense that *dhamma* as a moral principle is said to protect one who follows it.[13] "The goods follow the goods, the goods fill the goods, for the sake of moving from hither (suffering) to thither (happiness, freedom).[14] Objectivity understood in this sense requires no conception of permanence or eternality for its justification. It can replace the conception of *brahma*, the eternal and incorruptible moral law of the Brahmanical thinkers.

The second and third characteristics of the principle of dependence are necessity *(avitathatā)* and invariability *(anaññathatā)*. They are negative terms expressing the absence of arbitrariness and variableness. They are intended to preserve the concept of a principle without contradicting the idea of conditionality. This law-likeness, not absoluteness, implied by the term *dhammatā*, is used in a specifically moral sense in the *Discourse at Kosambi (Kosambiya-sutta)*.[15] Here the behavior of the moral person is explained in relation to several striking metaphors. One of them reads as follows

> Just as an innocent little baby lying on its back quickly draws back its hand or foot if it has touched a live ember, even so does a person possessed of moral rectitude *(dhammatā)* and endowed with a correct perspective *(diṭṭhisampanna)*, whatever kind of offence that person commits, an offence from which a reprieve is perceptible, that person immediately reveals it to a teacher, to the wise ones or to the co-religionists, and having done so that person refrains from committing it in the future.

The passage does admit that even a person of moral standing can commit offenses. This is because no human is endowed with omniscience. There is always a possibility that a person, even with a proper perspective, may commit an offense as a result of not being able to anticipate every situation or condition. The inability to anticipate future conditions does not mean that such a person can commit heinous crimes, hence the warning that only the effect of actions for which a reprieve is perceptible can be eliminated through confession. This is the concept of conditionality *(idappaccayatā)* built into the entire theory of dependent arising.

The Buddha was attempting to accommodate two important ideas in his theory of dependent arising. The first was to formulate the conception of uniformity or regularity or naturalness without committing himself to a theory of permanence and absolute determinism. The second was to safeguard the theory of conditionality from undue skepticism and indeterminism. The philosophical atmosphere was already muddied by the absolutist theories, and it was no easy task to express his realization of radical nonsubstantialism. This dilemma prompted him to adopt the epistemological standpoint explained in Chapter 2.

One further requirement of this moral principle is the accommodation of changing circumstances, new situations, or what is popularly referred to in modern philosophy as possibilities. The Buddha avoided the path taken by Mahāvīra, who tried to account for every possibility and eventually had to claim omniscience (see Chapter 1). Instead, the Buddha was willing to make modifications in the principle itself when new situations occurred. However, since the principle was formulated on the basis of the observations of what had transpired, not on the assumption of what ought to be independent of experience, he assumed that the changes or modifications should reflect "maximum continuity and minimum jolt" in the principle.[16] This being a matter of extreme significance, the Buddha, before his death, advised his disciples that after his death they could, if they so desired, revoke some of the minor rules of discipline.[17] The *Vinaya Piṭaka* refers to several instances when the Buddha himself revoked certain rules that he had previously prescribed for the monks.[18] In so doing he exemplified his view that the morals as well as the moral principle are like rafts.

CHAPTER 11

Justification of the Moral Life

Life without Permanence

After denying a permanent and ultimate reality in the world of human experience, and having declared that all becoming *(bhava)* is impermanent and nonsubstantial, the Buddha was not willing to accommodate any conception of permanence even as a rational requirement for the moral life. His conception of life or living beings is embodied in the theory of the five destinies *(pañca-gati)*.[1] They are the gods *(deva)* or the denizens of the various heavens *(sagga)*, the humans *(manussā)*, the hellish beings *(nerayika)* inhabiting the various hells *(niraya)*, those of the animal kingdom *(tiracchāṇayoni)*, and the departed spirits *(peta)*. The first two are generally looked upon as good destinies *(sugati)*, while the last three are described as bad destinies *(duggati)*. These five are not hierarchical, with the heavens at the top and the world of the departed spirits at the bottom. As will be explained later, they revolve with the world of humans at the center.

The Heavens

Several heavenly abodes are mentioned: the Cātummahārājikas, the Tāvatiṃsas, the Yamas, the Tusitas, the Nimmāṇaratis, the Paranimmitavasavattis, Brahmakāyikas, and those above them *(taduttari)*.[2] But none of them are permanent and eternal, even though life in the heavens is considered to be longer when compared with that of the humans. A human being who has led a virtuous life is born in these heavens. Thus, we have Sakka (Vedic, Indra) reborn as chief among the gods as a result of practicing simple virtues while he was a human being *(manussabhūta)*.[3]

Once the Buddha is represented as ridiculing Sakka for making too excessive a claim regarding morals.[4] Sakka is not free from birth, decay, death, sorrow, lamentation, pain, dejection, and dispair because he has not totally eradicated attachment, aversion, and confusion, whereas the Buddha's disciples, who have attained freedom from these, can claim moral superiority. The relationship between the virtuous life in the human world and the enjoyment of heavenly pleasures is expressed in a subtle way when it is said that the gods of the Tāvatiṃsa become agitated when their flock is reduced as a result of human beings not practicing the virtues.[5]

Reaching the company of Brahmā *(brahmasahavyatā)* is no doubt an allusion to the Upaniṣadic ideal of attaining unity with *brahma,* the ultimate moral reality from which the three lower social classes are derived. The Buddha's own version of reaching the company of Brahmā or being born in the world of Brahmā is therefore based upon the practice of four socially significant virtues, namely, friendliness, compassion, rejoicing (in the happiness of others), and equanimity, but not the fulfilling of duties assigned by caste. The Buddha claimed that in some of his previous lives he considered the attainment of the company of Brahma as the moral ideal and that he instructed his disciples on how to achieve it. However, in this life he realized that it is only a halfway house.[6] Therefore, he found fault with Sāriputta for instructing a brahman named Dhanañjāni, while he lay on his deathbed, regarding the way to the Brahmā world, when he could have been directed at a higher achievement *(uttariṃ karaṇīya),* which is cessation of birth. Sāriputta's response was that the brahmans are intent on the ideal of reaching Brahmā.[7] There indeed are references to the world of Brahmā becoming empty.[8] The possibility was recognized that the gods could fall from heaven straight into any one of the three lower realms.[9] The best possible destiny for the gods is said to be birth in the human realm. A discourse in the *Itivuttaka*[10] describes how the gods who found one of their kind ready to pass away from heaven *(devakāyā cavanadhammo)* exhorted him to be reborn in a good destiny *(sugati),* obtain a good acquisition, and be well established. Questioned by a monk as to what these three are, the Buddha responded by saying that a good destiny for such a person is birth as a human *(manussatta),* a good acquisition is having the opportunity to place confidence *(saddhā)* in the teachings of the Buddha, and to be well established is to have confidence in the teachings.

Bad Destinies (Duggati)

The sufferings in hell are graphically described in a passage in the *Aṅguttara-nikāya.*[11] The concept of Yama, who, according to Vedic mythology, was the first departed ancestor of the humans, was adopted by the Buddha as the sovereign who decides what form of punishment should be meted out to evildoers immediately after their deaths. Yama is supposed to send his divine messengers *(devadūta),* symbolizing old age, decay, disease, and death, and the human beings who ignored them and continued to commit evil deeds are then subjected to the most severe punishments by the guardians of hell *(nirayapāla).*

While the excruciating pain and suffering one undergoes in hell are described in the discourses, no comparable descriptions are found of the sufferings of animals and the departed spirits. It is only in a later text, the *Petavatthu,* a text that received canonical status sometime before the canon came to be closed, that we find the accounts of the sufferings of the departed spirits. Several reasons may be adduced for this. First, the sufferings of animals are too obvious. Unlike the hells or the world of the departed spirits, the animal world is physically available for the humans to perceive. Second, the world of the departed spirits *(peta),* traceable to the pre-Buddhist concept of the departed ancestors, is looked upon with more sympathy than that of those who suffer in the hells. On the one hand, they are one's own relatives, and on the other, the evils committed by them are mostly in the form of being miserly, selfish, and greedy. They did not commit evil deeds comparable to those of the denizens of hell. Thus, the departed spirits become not only objects of human sympathy, but also subjects of human generosity, the nonpractice of which brought about their unfortunate destiny. The *Petavatthu* emphasizes the extent to which the departed spirits depend upon their living relatives to free them from their sufferings. That this was a strong incentive for the moral life is exemplified by its prevalence in places like China and Japan even before the introduction of Buddhism. This belief gave rise to various rituals, such as offering gifts *(dakkhiṇā)* to the monks and nuns and transferring the merit thereof to the departed spirits.[12] Here again, by recognizing the fact that the departed ancestors can benefit by the generosity of living relatives and return to life as humans, the Buddha was making human life the center of the universe.

The question as to whether heavens, hells, or the world of departed spirits are real in the sense that humans and animals are real is one that would generally be raised by the skeptical materialist thinker, as was done during the Buddha's day. For the psychologist Buddha, these places are not unreal; they are real in the sense of depicting the most exotic pleasures and the most excruciating pain one can suffer even as humans.[13] It is consistent with the idea that the Buddha continued to emphasize—that within this fathom-long body associated with consciousness and mind is the world, its arising, its cessation, and the path leading to its cessation.[14]

It seems that the Buddha focused his attention on life without hellish sufferings and heavenly frustrations, a middle path that was discussed earlier. From the material presented in Chapters 6–9, it is evident that, according to the Buddha, the virtues and morals differ in terms of their scope. The virtues represent the beginning of the moral life, which is intended to bring about social harmony, while the morals are more comprehensive in that they are concerned with the ultimate health, both physical and mental, and the welfare of oneself and others. Thus, the fruits of the virtuous life and the moral life need not be identical. It was therefore possible for the Buddha to offer heavenly pleasures as the reward for virtues, even though in the larger or more exalted context of morals those pleasures themselves serve as obstructing conditions *(antarāyikā dhammā)*.[15] The stories about heavens in the early discourses illustrate precisely this fact.

In presenting the five destinies in the above manner, and recognizing no other destiny, the Buddha was working within the context of human life. The four destinies surrounding human life are satellites that facilitate moral discourse. Moral progress does not stretch into an unchartered domain; it is within this human life and experience. Moral perfection is part of human life with the other four destinies benefitting from such perfection. Furthermore, the Buddha's doctrines of karma and rebirth are embodied in this description. Therefore, it may be appropriate to examine them in some detail so that some of the misunderstandings can be cleared before they are presented as justifications for the moral life.

Karma

Among the various reasons we become involved in discussions of human action, there seem to be two very important ones. First, there is an interest in the consequences of action, mostly because we like to know whether an action will lead to happiness or suffering. Second, there is a need to determine who or what is responsible for the action, and this involves us in the examination of sources or motives of action. These two issues are therefore present in various forms in the theories of action. Thus, in the Buddhist context, the term karma, while signifying an individual action, is also used to refer to the doctrine of karma involving a relation between action and consequence.

The Buddha's discourses refer to four types of theories presented by his predecessors and contemporaries. First, an action is performed by oneself and, as such, the consequences, whether good or bad, are also reaped solely by oneself. This is the early Brahmanical theory, with its *ātma*-metaphysic (i.e., the one that prevailed before the appearance of the idea in the *Bhagavadgītā* that in the final analysis a human is only an instrument [*nimitta*] of God). Second is the view that one person acts and another experiences the consequences. This seems like the theory presented by the biological determinists, who denied the efficacy of human action but maintained that all beings experience happiness and suffering as a result of biological evolution, a process that is external to the beings. Third is a combination of the first two views, which is the theory adopted by the Jainas. It combined the metaphysics of the first two and, as a result, turned out to be the most deterministic theory of karma. Fourth is a theory that rejected the previous theories and argued that everything in the world, including happiness and suffering, is accidental *(adhiccasamuppanna)*.[16]

None of these theories was compatible with what the Buddha realized to be the nature of existence, or becoming. In his own formulation of the theory of action he had to accommodate many issues that were compatible with his insight and understanding. For example, there could not be absolute certainty regarding the connection between action and consequence, but that did not mean they are totally unrelated. The relationship had to be conditional because no two situations in which an action is performed are identical. The concept of a self was important, but such a self could not be eternal and immutable. External factors would play a role, but even they are not the sole determinants.

The most philosophical account of the doctrine of karma in Buddhism is found in the *Greater Discourse on the Analysis of Action (Mahākammavibhaṅga-sutta)*.[17] Here the Buddha refers to four kinds of persons:

1. One who has performed evil actions and is reborn in an evil state, in hell
2. One who has performed evil actions and is reborn in a good state, in heaven
3. One who has performed good actions and is reborn in a good state, in heaven
4. One who has performed good actions and is reborn in an evil state, in hell[18]

At first glance, this admission of the possibility of examples of two and four may appear to invalidate the doctrine of karma. However, the Buddha proceeds to explain that ascetics and brahmans who developed higher forms of knowledge when perceiving examples one and three asserted deterministic theories about karma by universalizing a relation between action and consequence. Similarly, by universalizing the absence of a relation between action and consequence in examples two and four, some arrived at theories of indeterminism.[19] Buddha's criticism here is twofold. First, after observing examples one and three or two and four, it is inappropriate to reach the conclusion that this is the case with regard to all *(sabba)*. A dogmatic adherence to any one set of observations, saying, "This alone is true; everything else is false" *(idam eva saccaṃ, moghaṃ aññaṃ)* is not epistemologically justified. Second, if someone has performed evil actions here and now *(idha)* and is reborn in heaven, there is no need to immediately come to the conclusion that the doctrine of karma is invalid. For it is possible that the person had performed good actions in the past or, at the moment of death in this life, cultivated right views. In other words, to arrive at a deterministic theory that an evildoer is destined to be reborn in hell, it is necessary for us to have an absolutely perfect record of that person's behavior from the time of birth, if not before birth, until the moment of death. Such retrieval of information is not available even to the higher forms of knowledge such as clairvoyance, except omniscience, which the Buddha disclaimed. It is also possible that the consequences of evil actions may be reaped here in this life itself *(diṭṭhe va dhamme)* without having to wait for a future life. This latter qualification was of great significance, for it allows room for a person who has done evil in the past to attain enlightenment and freedom in this very life. The story of Aṅgulimāla, the murderer, is the best illustration of this idea.[20] A discourse included in the *Aṅguttara-nikāya*[21] represents a further commentary on this issue. Here, the Buddha says that if a person were to maintain that "just as a person does a deed, so does that person experience its consequences," then the living of the noble life would be rendered meaningless, for there would be no opportunity for the complete elimination of suffering (i.e., the attainment of *nibbāna*). But if one accepts the theory that "just as this person does a deed whose consequences would be determined in a certain way [lit., "a deed whose consequences is to be experienced in a certain way"], so does that person experience its consequences," then the noble life will be meaningful and there will be an opportunity for the complete elimination of suffering. The distinction drawn here is as follows: In the first case, there is complete determinism between action and consequence; in the second, the recognition of the circumstances in which the action is committed, and so on, makes the effect conditional upon the circumstances. This is illustrated by an apt metaphor. If a person threw a grain of salt into a small cup of water, the water in that cup would become salty and undrinkable because of that salt. If a person were to throw a similar grain of salt into the river Ganges, because of the great mass of water therein, the water would not become salty and undrinkable. Similarly, some trifling evil action of a person may lead him to hell. But a similar trifling evil action committed by another person may bring consequences experienced in this very life—consequences, indeed, that may be barely noticeable. Here we find two people performing similar actions but reaping consequences in different ways. Thus, the same discourse states

> A certain person has not properly cultivated his body, behavior, thought and intelligence, is inferior and insignificant and his life is short and miserable; of such a person . . . even a trifling evil action done leads him to hell. In the case of a person who has proper culture of the body, behavior, thought and intelligence, who is superior and not insignificant, and who is endowed with long life, the consequences of a similar evil

action are to be experienced in this very life, and sometimes may not appear at all.

Thus, the consequence of an action is not determined solely by the action itself, but also by many other factors, such as the nature of the person who is responsible for the action and the circumstances under which it is done. This again is an application of the Buddha's conception of dependent arising, or conditionality, to the explanation of human action.

Rebirth, or the Survival of the Human Personality

The Buddhist doctrine of rebirth, or the survival of the human personality, has generated much controversy among modern scholars. For the Buddhist scholar interested in interpreting the doctrine in the light of what he or she believes to be critical modern philosophy, the idea of rebirth is no more than an ancient Indian philosophical relic either let alone by the Buddha because it was supposed to do no harm or brought into the Buddhist fold by his later disciples. It was not the least compatible with the Buddha's conception of no-self or nonsubstantiality. For the traditional Buddhist scholar rebirth is an absolutely inevitable occurrence until a person attains enlightenment and freedom.

There are several important questions that need to be answered before leaping to any such conclusions. To what extent is the doctrine justified by the Buddha's epistemological assertions? How compatible is it with his conceptions of nonsubstantiality and dependent arising? What is it that connects a human life of the past with that of the present, or, to use a Buddhist technical term, what connects the two processes of becoming? What is the relevance of the doctrine to social and moral philosophy? We will try to answer these questions in that order.

We have already referred to the Buddha's recognition of certain forms of higher knowledge that are the products of deep meditative contemplations, especially retrocognition and clairvoyance. According to the discourses, retrocognition, which provides information about one's own survival, is simply a sharpened memory of certain events, situations, or associations of the past. The Buddha himself claimed that he remembered some of his past lives, and three specific ones are described in great detail.[22] Such memories have been reported even by those who did not practice yoga, especially by children during the early stages of their lives before their attention become focused on the present.[23] Clairvoyance, or the knowledge of the survival of others, does not involve memory. Hence, it has to deal with the moment of its occurrence. The description of this knowledge is therefore always given in the present tense. For example, it is said that the clairvoyant "sees beings ceasing and arising" *(satte passati cavamāne uppajjamāne).*[24] It is compared to the perception of someone who, standing in a high-rise, sees people leaving one house and entering another. Occasions on which the Buddha appeared at the scenes of the death of two of his disciples, Godhika[25] and Vakkhali,[26] are reported, and on both occasions he observed that they passed away without being reborn. Those who are brought up in the traditions that accept only the "one-life-after-death" theory are generally not inquisitive about where their loved ones would be after death. That one life is common to all. However, in the traditions that recognize rebirth, people are very much interested in finding out how their kith and kin fare after death. When the Buddha visited a place called Nādikā, Ānanda, probably goaded by the people of Nādikā, questioned the Buddha about the fate of the Nādikans who had died. The Buddha's response was that what happens to a person depends upon that person's character. The Buddha then presented them with what he called the "mirror of morals" *(dhammādāsa)* so that a person, without having to harass the Buddha with such questions, could look at oneself and predict about oneself *(attanā va attānaṃ vyākareyya)* where one would go after death.[27]

If there were an easy solution to the problem of rebirth, it would be accepting a permanent and eternal self, as did the Brahmanical tradition. The Buddha rejected that solution. His alternative explanation of rebirth is couched in the language of dependent arising, hence his statement that at least three conditions have to be fulfilled for a human to come into existence: the coitus of the parents, the mother being in the proper season, and the presence of a *gandhabba.*[28] The first two conditions are not controversial, while the third is.

Gandhabba is a metaphorical description of consciousness *(viññāṇa)* at the moment of death craving for survival *(bhavataṇhā),* hence the Buddha's statement that if consciousness were not to enter the mother's womb, the psychophysical personality or the living organism formed therein would not reach maturity.[29] The idea that the human mind, or consciousness, at the time of its first flickerings even before actual birth is a tabula rasa is not accepted by the Buddha. The reason is that the consciousness and the psychophysical personality *(nāmarūpa)* formed in the mother's womb are interdependent.[30] Apart from the findings of the most advanced research in neuroscience, which seem to support the idea that consciousness at this stage is not a tabula rasa, there are influential philosophers of the modern world who would admit that there is a possibility that one may pick up the memory of a dead person and maintain some continuity in the personality.[31]

It is generally believed that rebirth means an uninterrupted continuity of the entire personality from the previous life. If that were to happen, the human community would be faced with a rather incredible and awkward situation where human beings would be returning life after life to claim the properties they left behind in their previous lives. Preservation of the entire personality is what everyone dreams of, whether they believe in rebirth or in one life after death. What is surprising is that both philosophers and nonphilosophers are willing to accept memory as an important criterion for personal identity, even though some of the more sophisticated empiricists would insist upon the physical body as the only criterion.[32] It is difficult to see how a physical personality that has not remained unchanged can be the sole criterion for absolute identity. But what about memory? Does a memory that a person may have, say, of an event or of himself or herself provide justification for the belief in a permanent identity? The memory is not independent of the event or the person of that particular time, and both these would have changed considerably. The recognition of a memory trait independent of everything else associated with it gives the false impression of an unchanging identity. The memories themselves, along with the psychophysical frame within which they occur, are in a state of flux, and that flux is, to use the Buddha's language, "dependently arisen" *(paṭiccasamuppanna)*.[33] What may remain unchanged from the time a birth certificate is written until the death certificate is compiled is the "accidental word" (*yadṛcchā-śabda;* i.e., the proper name, according to Dignāga) with which that frame came to be identified.

For the Buddha it may be one single memory associated with the context, a minute element out of a lifetime of experience, that can continue.

That memory can then mold the new personality. Even a later disciple, the famous Nāgārjuna, maintained that out of all the actions a person may perform during a lifetime, only one gets transferred at the time of rebirth.[34] However, such a transfer is dependent upon the availability of the other conditions mentioned earlier. There is no guarantee that all these conditions will be met. Thus, the early discourses do not maintain that every person who dies is sure to be reborn. All that is asserted is that past cases of survival have been observed and it may occur in the future as well. This is how the theory of survival is accommodated under the theory of conditionality.

The Buddha was not unaware that unless a person develops the higher forms of knowledge such as retrocognition or clairvoyance, which enable a person to remember incidents of the past and perceive the survival of other beings, it would not be easy to convince oneself of the validity of the doctrines of karma and rebirth. Hence, they could not be used as arguments for convincing the ordinary people of the need to follow a moral life. In the absence of a strong imperative based upon either a moral Absolute or the belief in a Supreme Being or power whose omnipotence could induce the people to a moral life, in the absence of commandments of any sort but only advice to refrain from evil and to cultivate the good life, it would not be easy to encourage and urge ordinary people to adopt a moral life. The Buddha's strategy was to utilize the doctrines of karma and rebirth as a wager. This is the content of his dialogue with the villagers of Sāla recorded in the *Discourse on the Unquestionable (Apaṇṇaka-sutta).*[35]

The Buddha, attended by a large retinue of monks, was once visiting the country of the Kosalans and arrived at a brahman village called Sāla. The brahman householders heard about the arrival of the Buddha in their village. Having come to know of his reputation as an enlightened one and the nature of his teachings, they visited him and greeted him respectfully. The Buddha inquired of them as to whether they had some satisfactory teacher in whom they had reasonable confidence *(ākāravatī saddhā).* When they responded in the negative, the Buddha presented them with what can be called a "wager" on the moral life.

First he referred to three of the amoralist theories presented by the philosophers of the ascetic tradition (discussed in Chapter 1). These, in order, are the views attributed to Ajita Kesakambali, Pūraṇa Kassapa, and

Makkhali Gosāla. The ideas of these philosophers were selected for discussion not only because they denied the validity of the moral life, but also because they rejected the efficacy of human effort as well as the conceptions of karma and survival. The recognition of the efficacy of human effort was of paramount importance to the Buddha.

The Buddha presented them with the views of the amoralists mentioned above as well as views held by other ascetics and brahmans that were directly opposed to them. For example, he states the views attributed to Ajita

> There are, householders, some ascetics and brahmans who speak thus and who view thus: "There is no gift, there is no offering, there is no sacrifice, there is no fruit or ripening of action well done or ill done, this world does not exist, a world beyond does not exist, there is no mother, there is no father, there are no beings of spontaneous birth, in this world there are no ascetics and brahmans, well-gone, well-behaved and who know this world and the world beyond through their own higher knowledge and realization.

The Buddha then presented the view of other ascetics and brahmans who asserted everything that is negated in the above passage. Having done so, he questioned the people of Sāla as to why the former group of ascetics and brahmans performed evil actions of body, speech, and mind after renouncing good and wholesome actions. Their response was that these ascetics and brahmans did not know the evil effects of evil actions and the good effects of good actions. The response of the people of Sāla can be taken as a natural one. They did not have a teacher who could teach them metaphysics. Yet they certainly were aware of some of the basic morals recognized in an ordinary society. However, they lacked any strong conviction about such morals or any justification for adopting them, hence the Buddha's decision to throw a wager, a proposition that is not questionable *(apaṇṇaka)*. Referring to a person who does evil and does not believe in retribution in an afterlife, the Buddha said

> Herein, householders, an intelligent person reflects thus: "If there is no world beyond, this worthy individual, at the break up of the body, after death will be safe. However, if there were to be a world beyond, this worthy individual, at the break up of the body, after death, will be reborn in purgatory, evil bourn, a fallen state, hell. Let it be that there is

> no world beyond, let the words of these ascetics and brahmans be true, yet this person in this very life will earn the contempt of the intelligent ones: 'This person is of bad virtues, of confused views, is nihilistic.' However, if there were to be a world beyond, then this person will face calamity in both ways: the contempt of the intelligent ones in this life and, after death, rebirth in purgatory, evil bourn, fallen state, hell. Thus, this unquestionable idea has been imperfectly grasped by him, remains partially touched and thereby looses the wholesome position."[36]

It is interesting to note that this wager is a little different from that of Blaise Pascal, which he formulated centuries later. The reason is that Pascal's wager emphasized what happens to the nonbeliever after death if God were to exist. The Buddha's argument focused not only on the evil consequences an evil person would reap if there were to be an afterlife, but also on what he or she would experience in this life *(diṭṭhe va dhamme)* as well, namely, the condemnation by the intelligent ones. Thus, the immoral one faces calamity in two ways *(ubhayattha kaliggaho).* It may be that the addition of a second consequence was needed because, unlike the concept of God, which is absolute, the Buddha's theory of rebirth, or survival, is conditional. His theory of survival did not guarantee that everyone who dies is reborn. Thus, while recognizing rebirth as a possibility, he was not willing to wager on that alone.

The doctrine of karma and rebirth as outlined above will not satisfy the moral skeptic. Arguably, these conceptions as propounded by the Buddha are too weak to encourage the adoption of the moral life. Realizing this, the Buddha was ready with another argument. Working through the theory of five destinies, the Buddha brought human life to the center of the stage. Placing human life in that context, the Buddha was now able to argue for its rarity. He emphasized this idea throughout the discourses, but one discourse stands out.[37] Obtaining birth as a human is rare and more difficult than the success on the part of a sea turtle, blind in one eye, to get its head through the hole of a single-hole yoke floating back and forth on the surface of the ocean, in order to get a glimpse of the open sky. Human life, in spite of its impermanence, unsatisfactoriness, and nonsubstantiality, is a precious opportunity not to be wasted away.

> Hard is the gain of human [life]; hard is the life of mortals; hard is the hearing of the good teaching and hard is the arising of enlightened ones.[38]

The Buddha's advice is to not let a moment pass by without achieving what can be achieved. Having gained such an opportunity, and being possessed of intelligence and abilities that surpass even those of the gods, it would be the highest folly not to strive for the happiness and welfare of oneself and others.

PART THREE

APPLICATIONS OF THE PRINCIPLE

CHAPTER 12

Society and Morals

I HAVE ALREADY pointed out how the Brahmanical theory of social organization determined its social ethic (see Chapter 1). According to this theory, the caste gradation is an absolute one, hence the obligation to abide by the duties of the caste. The Buddha considered it nothing but a relative division.[1] King Pasenadi of Kosala had to admit that in times of war he would be compelled to enlist capable young men irrespective of their castes. In another instance, the Buddha argued that a prosperous member of any caste would be able to employ members of each of the other castes to wait upon him or her.[2] The Buddha observed no distinction in terms of the striving or effort *(padhāna-vemattatā)* among the people of the different castes.[3]

The Buddha admitted that one of the conditions that could possibly determine one's birth into any caste is one's behaviour in a past life. Yet he was not willing to make it an absolute condition (see Chapter 11). More important for him than a previous karma is the karma of a person in this life in deciding a person's status in society.[4]

In contrast to the static conception of society advocated by the Brahmanical tradition, the Buddha, following his radical empiricism, presented an evolutionary view. He began with a fanciful account of the origin of the earth, as any account of the origin would be. After the earth had been formed, beings who managed to move to other planets while the earth was being destroyed return to earth. Vegetation of low, and then higher, grade evolved. This brought forth an abundance of cereals, and agricultural life emerged. Dependent upon this agriculture were the human families, who formed into households. As households developed, food began to be stored and land was divided among the individual owners. Setting up of boundaries gave rise to property rights. Someone too lazy to develop his or her property and of greedy disposition encroached upon another's property. The others would accuse him or her of trespass; thus, strife and injustice entered the life of humans. As the situation deteriorated, people got together and selected as ruler someone from among themselves who could command the respect of the others. The selection was based upon the people's consent; hence, the first ruler was named Mahāsammata (lit., "agreed to by the multitude"; i.e., "the Great Elect"). He was to maintain justice, and others provided him with all the support necessary. The king was referred to as the lord of the "field" *(khetta),* hence the term *khattiya (kṣatriya),* or ruler. Certain other humans, distressed at the growing social crimes and evils, retired into the forest to live a life of isolation and devoted themselves to meditation and other religious rituals. These were the *brāhmaṇas,* or priests. Most others spent their lives in households becoming proficient in some productive vocation. They became the *vessa (vaiśya),* the ordinary citizens. The remaining members of the society engaged themselves in minor or low vocations such as serving others and came to be known as the *sudda (śūdra).*[5]

Commenting on this fanciful account of the evolution of the society and the responsibilities of its members, Rhys Davids remarked, "In spite of its good humoured irony and its fanciful etymologies, the discourse reveals a sound and healthy insight [into social evolution] and is much nearer to the actual facts than the brahmin legend it was intended to replace."[6] The important point made in the discourse is that the social and functional differences among human beings came about as a result of "self-interest" being pitted against what I previously referred to as "mutual self-interest", that is, the collective interest of society. The social ethic is therefore not an absolute one decreed from above or outside, but one that evolved catering to the well-being of the social group. It is the *dhamma.* Anything that is detrimental to the well-being of the social group is *adhamma,* or evil.

Observe that the evolution described here is not a linear one. In fact, the discourse begins by referring to the long alternate periods of dissolution *(saṃvaṭṭa)* and evolution *(vivaṭṭa).* It is cyclic, and this cyclic dissolution-evolution-dissolution process takes place in terms of dependent arising.

Society, according to the Buddha, is subject to three natural disabilities or diseases *(ābādha):* desire *(icchā),* hunger *(anasanaṃ),* and decay *(jarā).*[7] In the context of a theory that recognizes mutual self-interest or collective human interest as the definition of society, human desire can be the most potent cause of social ill. For the so-called scientific sociologist, this is merely a psychological factor having no relevance to the evolution and function of society. For the Buddha, the effect of greed on the social life of human beings is devastating. It is the "disease of mind" *(cetasika roga)*[8] that can destroy the moral fabric of the society. Hunger is a physical or an economic disease that can be alleviated not by allowing the first kind of disease to prevail, that is, by permitting the overproduction of food items prompted by greed on the part of the producer, but by following a middle path of catering to the needs of a restrained society. Decay is an existential disease, that is, one that is part of existence, which is subject to arising and ceasing. Social institutions are not immune to decay and destruction. Continued restructuring or organizing of social institutions, taking into consideration the winds of change, provides for a healthy society. The Buddha did precisely this with the organization that he founded, namely, the community of monks and nuns (see Chapter 15). However, there must be some principle under which such restructuring should take place. That principle, as explained earlier (see Chapter 10), is the welfare of oneself and others, that is, mutual self-interest.

The best account of this concept of society based on mutual human interest is found in the *Discourse on the Admonition to Sigāla (Sigālovāda-suttanta).*[9] The Buddha once came across a person named Sigāla, who, rising early morning, cleansing his hair, and donning clean garments, was worshipping the six directions, east, west, north, south, nadir, and zenith. Upon inquiry, the Buddha found out that Sigāla performed this ritual daily because his father, on his deathbed, advised him to do so. The Buddha's admonition is quoted in full because it provides the best account of the rights and responsibilities of the individuals in a society.

> And, how, householder's son, does the Aryan disciple protect the six directions? These six things are to be regarded as the six directions. The east denotes mother and father. The south denotes teachers. The west denotes wife and children. The north denotes friends and companions. The nadir denotes servants, workers and helpers. The zenith denotes ascetics and brahmans.

There are five ways in which a son should administer to his mother and father as the eastern direction. [He should think:] "Having been supported by them, I will support them. I will perform their duties for them. I will keep up the family tradition. I will be worthy of my heritage. After my parents' deaths I will distribute gifts on their behalf." And there are five ways in which the parents, so ministered to by their son as the eastern direction, will reciprocate: they will restrain him from evil, support him in doing good, teach him some skill, find him a suitable wife and, in due time, hand over his inheritance to him. In this way the eastern direction is covered, making it at peace and free from fear.

There are five ways in which pupils should minister to their teachers as the southern direction: by rising to greet them, by waiting on them, by being attentive, by serving them, by mastering the skills they teach. And there are five ways in which their teachers, thus ministered to by the pupils as the southern direction, will reciprocate: they will give thorough instruction, make sure that they have duly grasped what they should have duly grasped, give them a thorough grounding in all skills, recommend them to their friends and colleagues, and provide them with security in all directions. In this way the southern direction is covered, making it at peace and free from fear.

There are five ways in which a husband should minister to his wife as the western direction: by honoring her, by not disparaging her, by not being unfaithful to her, by giving authority to her, by providing her with adornments. And there are five ways in which a wife, thus ministered to by her husband as the western direction, will reciprocate: by properly organizing her work, by being kind to the servants, by not being unfaithful, by protecting stores, and by being skillful and diligent in all she has to do. In this way the western direction is covered, making it at peace and free from fear.

There are five ways in which a man should minister to his friends and companions as the northern direction: by gifts, by kindly words, by looking after their welfare, by treating them like himself, and by keeping his word. And there are five ways in which friends and companions, thus ministered to by a man as the northern direction, will reciprocate: by looking after him when he is inattentive, by looking after his property when he is inattentive, by being a refuge when he is afraid, by not deserting him when he is in trouble, and by showing concern for his children. In this way the northern direction is covered, making it at peace and free from fear.

There are five ways in which a master should minister to his servants

> and workpeople as the nadir: by arranging their work according to their strength, by supplying them with food and wages, by looking after them when they are ill, by sharing special delicacies with them, and by letting them off work at the right time. And there are five ways in which servants and workpeople, thus ministered to by their master as the nadir, will reciprocate: they will get up before him, go to bed after him, take only what they are given, do their work properly, and be bearers of his praise and good repute. In this way the nadir is covered, making it at peace and free from fear.
>
> There are five ways in which a man should minister to ascetics and brahmans as the zenith: by kindness in bodily deed, speech and thought, by keeping open house for them, by supplying their bodily needs. And the ascetics and brahmans, thus ministered to by him as the zenith, will reciprocate in six ways: they will restrain him from evil, encourage him to do good, be benevolently compassionate towards him, teach him what he has not heard, and point out to him the way to heaven. In this way the zenith is covered, making it at peace and free from fear.[10]

Here we have a broad spectrum of relations, found in most societies. One may be reminded of the Confucian doctrine of filial piety. However, there are two major differences between the two theories. An important component in the Confucian list is the relationship between the ruler and the ruled. Political instability in early China prompted the philosophers to focus on political philosophy. Compared to China, the Indian continent was politically more stable, hence the noninclusion of the ruler-ruled relationship. The second major difference is that at this time India was teeming with religious teachers, ascetics, and brahmans, and the mutual relationship between the householder and the religious teacher was of great importance. This is in contrast to the Chinese situation, where until the introduction of Buddhism religious teachers did not constitute a significant or recognizable segment of society.

Several important features stand out in the detailed description of mutual relations set out in the above passage. It begins with the micro-unit of the society, namely, the family. Without harmonious and healthy families there cannot be a healthy society. The mutual responsibilities of the parents and children include not only looking after and nurturing one another, but also taking care of their moral and religious welfare. The pursuit of the happiness and welfare of oneself and others, the foundation of the Buddha's moral philosophy, is inculcated in every form of relationship, whether it be between parents and children, husband and wife, teacher and pupil, religious and laypersons, master and servant, or among friends. Benevolence and compassion are the most important sentiments inspiring each person's behavior.

Finally, the Buddhist conception of society is not confined to humans. In a profound ethical sense it includes all living beings *(sabbabhūta)*, animals as well as lower creatures. "As a mother who protects her own child as her own life, so should one develop thoughts toward all living beings."[11] In addition to the virtues discussed earlier, which invlove compassion for all forms of living beings, there are four mental states one is supposed to cultivate, and these, as mentioned in Chapter 5, include friendliness *(mettā)*, compassion *(karuṇā)*, rejoicing in the happiness of others *(muditā)*, and equanimity *(upekkhā)*, and carry a special designation as the "noble way of life" *(brahmavihāra)*.[12]

CHAPTER 13

Economics and Morals

A MODERN STUDENT of philosophy may find a discussion of economics irrelevant to ethical theory. In the traditional Western textbooks on ethics one hardly finds a chapter dealing with economics and morals. The reason for this is that modern philosophers have generally distinguished the moral life from the good life.[1] They are made to be so incompatible that if one were to have a good life one would have to sacrifice morals, and if one were to be moral, one would have to abandon the good life. In other words, the moral life has to override the good life. Ultimate questions in ethics therefore have nothing to do with economics, which is the foundation of the good life.

It is possible to discover at least two important reasons for this attitude. One has already been discussed: the Glaucon syndrome, which identifies any and every form of self-interest as being incompatible with morals. The moral ideal is polluted by the minutest element of self-interest, self-sacrifice being the foundation of morality. The second reason is the dominance of crass utilitarianism and materialism in the field of economics. The enormous developments in science and technology, all dominated by materialist thinking, in the modern world gave a new twist to economics never before seen in the world. Economics became a science with universal prosperity as a goal. The moral life once again became a pollutant of the good life based upon the scientific and technological developments. One of the leading economists of the twentieth century who broke ranks with the economic gurus is E. F. Schumacher. His epoch-making work, *Small is Beautiful. Economics as if People Mattered* (1973), already translated into several languages, is an extremely well-argued and well-substantiated piece that demonstrates how unbridled scientific and technological developments that helped the production of material goods at an unprecedented scale have led to global problems relating to the environment, society, and morals. Although 90 percent of the work is on economics, it could be considered a revolutionary work on morals and society. Schumacher's constant reference is to the cry of the modern-day economists to postpone the practice of morals until the good life has been achieved and enjoyed.

Although materialist thinking did not dominate the Indian lifestyle as it did in the modern world, the moral philosophy outlined above was part of Indian thought and practice even during the time of the Buddha. The theory of the stages of life favored by the ascetic tradition, in contrast to the deontology based on the caste system, fostered ideas similar to those prevailing among economists today. It prescribed duties for the people on a graduated level; the strictly moral or spiritual duties, other than performing simple sacrifices, were confined to a later period of one's life. Kauṭilya's *Arthaśāstra* (lit., a treatise on economics) presents a political theory based primarily on materialistic economics, with spiritualism tagged onto it as an ideal. Material progress, measured by the royal granary as well as the production of arms and so on, was the source of the king's authority and power.

We need to examine the Buddha's conception of the economic life of human beings in this background. The most comprehensive discussion of it is found in the *Discourse on the Lion's Roar of a Universal Monarch (Cakkavattisīhanāda-suttanta)*.[2] It refers to a Universal Monarch, coming after a long line of such monarchs whose authority rested on their being righteous *(dhammika)*, who decided to rule the people according to his own wishes. The result was a breakdown in law and order. In consultation with the ministers and counselors, the king instituted righteous means of security, protection, and guard for the people but did not take any measures to improve their economic conditions. In other words, he did not create opportunities for the people to acquire wealth *(dhana)*. When there were no such opportunities, poverty *(daliddiya)* became rampant. Normally it is assumed that "power corrupts." In this case, it was poverty that corrupted the people. Those who did not have the basic necessities of life resorted to stealing. To avoid punishment they were compelled to commit other evils such as lying. One may assume that since Buddhism contributed to the doctrine of karma it is compelled to attribute poverty to lack of initiative or entrepreneurship on the part of the person; it is the karma of that person. But this initial passage in the discourse places the blame not on the individual, but on the society that prevented the individual from having an opportunity. Many Buddhist scholars have utilized this passage to argue that Buddhism supports communism in its assertion that maldistribution of wealth is the cause of all the evils in society. This certainly is not the intent of the discourse. The passage is simply an admission that a comfortable material life is an important factor contributing toward a harmonious social life. There cannot be harmony when the belly is empty. However, the discourse goes on to maintain that merely providing opportunities for making a comfortable living is not sufficient in itself. According to the Buddha, no two human beings are born equal. In addition to the differences in the physical constitution, there are also differences regarding temperaments, dispositions, and so on.

Thus, when a person resorted to stealing because of the lack of the basic amenities of life, the king decided to provide him with the opportunity to acquire some wealth. Others in similar positions who heard about it resorted to stealing in the hope of gaining the king's favor. Finally, when the situation was out of control, the king had to mete out severe punishment for stealing and other crimes. This is another point made in Buddhist economics: equal distribution of wealth alone does not solve economic and social problems. It has to go hand in hand with moral progress. In this context the virtues and morals discussed earlier come into play.

The Buddha's attitude toward material wealth was not different from his attitude toward sense experience, discussed earlier. When it is said that bondage and suffering are the result of our way of perceiving and conceiving the world, it does not mean that we have to do away with these two sources of knowledge and adopt a nonsensuous and nonconceptual intuition. The solution lies in the elimination of that aspect of perception and conception, that is, obsession, which causes bondage and suffering. I have also emphasized the idea that this obsession is not the result of simple human interest, but the outcome of desire. The Buddha carefully distinguished between human need and human greed. Similarly, material wealth or comfort is not in itself an evil. Abject poverty and deprivation are not the solutions to the problems caused by material wealth. Rather, it is the attachment to material wealth that is the source of the problem. Hence, the Buddha's statement, "Riches *(bhoga)* destroy the imprudent, but not verily those who seek the further shore," is immediately qualified by another: "Through craving for riches *(bhogataṇhā)*, the imprudent person destroys himself as though destroying others."[3] In fact, the fate of those who have not acquired some wealth during their prime is beautifully described in the following passage:

> Without having lived the noble life and without having acquired wealth in their prime, (some) languish like decrepit cranes in a lake depleted of fish.
>
> Without having lived the noble life and without having acquired wealth in their prime, (some) lie like overspent arrows, lamenting over things of the past.[4]

How the moral life and the acquisition of wealth can go together is best explained by the Buddha when he addressed Anāthapiṇḍika, a wealthy merchant who was a benefactor of the Buddha and his disciples. The Buddha spoke of four forms of happiness a layperson can enjoy: the realization that one has wealth *(atthi-sukha)*, the enjoyment of wealth *(bhoga-sukha)*, debtlessness *(anaṇa-sukha)*, and blamelessness *(anavajja-sukha)*.[5] What is significant is the nature of this wealth, which is said to be something earned through industry *(uṭṭhānaviriya)*, strength of the arms *(bāhābala)*, and sweat of the brow *(sedāvakkhitta)*, and through righteous means *(dhammika, dhammaladdha)*.

The introduction of the term righteous to define the means of acquiring wealth indicates that at every stage of that process a person needs to be morally concerned. The ultimate criterion of morality, it was mentioned, is the happiness of both oneself and others. When we speak of oneself and others, it could be a reference to oneself and other humans or oneself and other living beings, not necessarily humans, but animals as well. Righteous acquisition of wealth would therefore be twofold, depending upon which definition we adopt. If we take the first definition, then the acquisition of wealth, the economic activities such as the production of goods, should be for the welfare and happiness of humans. The welfare of humans would not be achieved by creating situations promoting greed and possessiveness. When the goods are produced without much concern for the human consumer, it is done purely for the sake of profit. This would increase greed on the part of the producer. It also would mean the production of goods that would generate lust, desire, and longing instead of satisfying the needs. This is what the Buddha called the "wealth generative of the strands of desire" *(kāmaguṇabhoga)*.[6]

If we adopt the second definition of oneself and others, then the so-called righteous wealth or economic progress needs to take into account the welfare of humans as well as animals. This is where the larger issue of a healthy environment *(paṭirūpadesa)* comes up. A healthy environment includes the social as well as the physical. The social environment has already been discussed. Safeguarding the physical environment was also of great concern to the Buddha. The place where he met with his disciples for discussion of the doctrine is generally called *ārāma,* a term for garden or grove (lit., a delightful place). Many such gardens were offered to the Buddha and his disciples, the most famous being Jeta's forest grove *(Jetavanārāma)* presented by Anāthapiṇḍika. Those who planted trees in the gardens or in the forest *(vana)* (the latter probably refers to the preservation of the forest) were considered people established in morals *(dhammaṭṭha)* and possessed of virtues *(sīlasampanna)*.[7] The term *ārāma* subsequently came to mean a temple, and the original meaning of the term also was preserved when all kinds of fruit trees were planted on the temple premises. How the disciples who had attained freedom enjoyed the beauty of the forest teeming with animals is explained in the *Theragāthā*.[8] A forest is recommended as a peaceful place where one can enjoy a moment of solitude.[9] Large-scale destruction of forests currently taking place in the name of economic development would therefore not be compatible with the righteous wealth that the Buddha advocated. Schumacher's chapter entitled "Buddhist Economics" is an excellent comparison of the Buddha's middle path and the present-day economic theories that are supposed to improve the so-called "standard of living" of human beings.[10]

The Universal Monarch is therefore one who is concerned not only with the material welfare of his subjects, but also their moral well-being. Hence, he is called upon to instruct the subjects on both economic welfare and moral development.[11] As such, a typical Buddhist treatise on economics would have to be called *Arthadharmaśāstra* (a treatise on economics and morals) instead of *Arthaśāstra* (a treatise on economics).

CHAPTER 14

Politics and Morals

THE DISCOURSES vouch for the existence of two forms of government during the Buddha's day: monarchism and republicanism.

The Brahmanical tradition provided the philosophical foundation for monarchy. During the early stages, the concept of duty was more or less part of a social and political doctrine rather than a religious one as it came to be developed in the *Bhagavadgītā*. The brahman priest served as the spiritual guide for the ruler and was often consulted on matters pertaining to philosophy, especially the morals of governance. In this capacity the brahman priest wielded much power. The term for the royal counselor was *purohita,* which literally means "one who is placed in front." The Buddha's own father, King Suddhodana, had a brahman counselor named Asita Kāladevala, who was proficient in all forms of traditional learning. We read of King Pasenadi of Kosala, even during a brief sojourn in a small township called Toraṇavatthu, looking for an ascetic or brahman whom he could consult.[1]

The existence of the republican form of government is attested to by the references to the Vajjians in the discourses.[2] The Brahmanical caste system, with its strong discrimination against some segments of the society, could not have provided philosophical justification for this form of government. I have provided evidence that points toward the existence of another strain of thought in India different from the more popular deontology: utilitarianism (see Chapter 1). Those who followed the utilitarian trend of thought could have been the supporters of republicanism. In fact, when the Buddha spoke of the Vajjians, he was not recommending a new set of principles that they should follow. He was inquiring whether the Vajjians were following the principles they had adopted previously. He was simply arguing that if they did so, they could not be harmed by King Ajātasattu. He even recommended that the monks and nuns adopt such principles.[3]

The fact that he spoke in favor of republicanism does not mean that he condemned every other form of government, including the monarchical. He clearly saw that a republican form of government would be beneficial to the monks and nuns who were educated and who were committed to following the moral principles. Republicanism could work better in such a society. He also seems to have realized that where the constituents were not so morally committed, a monarchical government could be more effective. It is for these reasons that the Buddha, while refusing to appoint a central authority to govern the monks and nuns, but allowing them to function as a democratic institution,[4] formulated a conception of an ideal king—a Universal Monarch *(cakkavatti)*. The *Discourse on the Lion's Roar of a Universal Monarch*[5] provides the most detailed account of the Buddha's conception of kingship. A careful examination of this conception of monarchy will reveal that it avoids the unfortunate aspects of the traditional Indian theory of monarchy and combines it with some form of republicanism.

First the unfortunate aspects of traditional monarchy. The Brahmanical tradition, through its conception of caste, first established the idea that a king is a king by virtue of being born into a royal family, that is, the warrior caste. Yet the freedom of the king was completely curtailed when the brahman priests took over the important function of counselor. They assumed the status of the indisputable guides of the king. The king became a puppet in the hands of the priest, and the general public had no say whatsoever in matters relating to the governance of the society.

Under the influence of the Brahmanical tradition the monarch was also empowered to mete out the most severe punishments to evildoers, irrespective of the conditions and circumstances in which a person committed evil actions. A person had to pay for his or her karma even with life.

Large-scale sacrifices were undertaken by the kings at the instigation of the priests. These involved wanton destruction of animal life, and these sacrifices caused untold suffering for the subjects who were compelled to prepare for them. The discourses refer to such sacrifices, especially one performed by King Pasenadi.[6]

It is in this context that the Buddha presented his conception of a Universal Monarch. I have already referred to the fanciful account of the evolution of the world and how the first king came to be selected. A Universal Monarch is depicted as one who sets rolling *(pavatteti)* a wheel *(cakka)* of human prosperity, just as the Buddha is said to have set rolling the wheel of righteousness *(dhammacakka)* with his first sermon at Kusinārā.[7] The wheel, which has become a symbol of Buddhism since the time of the great Indian emperor, Aśoka, has much philosophical significance. It does not stand for the idea of static permanence; it is the most appropriate representation of movement and change. The better the wheel is, the smoother and more comfortable the movement is. I have already emphasized the idea that principles of explanation, whether in the sphere of the physical, psychological, social, political, moral, or even linguistic, do not represent permanent and eternal laws. In all these there are changes, modifications, and improvements, and it is precisely this movement that is represented by the wheel. While the Buddha is the one who sets rolling the wheel of righteousness, the king is supposed to roll the wheel of prosperity, both material and moral, in a way that is beneficial to his subjects. When he is unable to do so his authority to rule disappears. This is when the wheel is said to disappear *(osakkati, ṭhānā cavati)* until the emergence of another Universal Monarch.[8]

It is natural for someone born into a royal family to be selected king, whatever the circumstances under which that royal lineage came to be accepted by the people. Karma of a past life is not completely discounted in explaining the fortunate circumstances in which one is born.[9] However, birth into a royal family does not by itself qualify a person to be king. Thus, we are told that when an old monarch decided to abdicate, he summoned his son, assigned him all the royal responsibilities, handed over all the regal paraphernalia, and left the household for a life in the forest in order to pursue the moral life leading to enlightenment and freedom. After seven days the new king's "divine gem of the wheel" *(dibbaṃ cakkaratanaṃ)*, or his authority to rule, disappeared. The king was disappointed and visited his father in the forest to complain about the disappearance of the wheel. The father's immediate response was that the wheel is not a "paternal heritage" *(pettikam dāyajjam)*.[10]

If the authority to rule is not a paternal or family heritage, then it has to be earned. This is where the old king instructed his son regarding the way of life of a Universal Monarch *(cakkavattivatta)*, which would restore his authority. It is a life of righteousness whereby he would provide righteous ward and protection *(dhammikaṃ rakkhāvaraṇaguttiṃ)* for all the subjects, including the army, those associated with the warriors, the householders, the villagers, those living in the provinces, ascetics, and brahmans, as well as the beasts of the forest *(miga)* and the birds of the air *(pakkhi).* He was to frequently consult with the ascetics and brahmans, who were devoted to a life of piety, on questions relating to what is good and bad. The regained wheel, when annointed, would start rolling in every direction, and even the king's adversaries would accept his authority.[11] Thus, it is a life of righteousness as well as one devoted to the welfare of the subjects—not birth alone—that accounts for the authority of a king.

The discourse also refers to another instance when, after the retirement of the old monarch, his son took over the reins. As in the previous case, within seven days the wheel disappeared. This time the young monarch decided to rule according to his own wishes *(samatena).* His rule did not bring about prosperity to the people. People advised him to consult with the ministers *(amacca),* who were knowledgeable about the way of a Universal Monarch. This highlights another important aspect of the Buddha's conception of monarchy: it is not a governance by a single individual. Nor is the king a mere titular head or a puppet. He represents a unity, not an individuality. His authority comes from below, from the people, not from above.

This latter idea leads us to the most significant characteristic of the Buddha's theory of government. If the authority to rule is derived from the people, then those very people could not be sacrificed in the name of law. The Universal Monarch is, therefore, expected to rule the country without harsh punishment and weapons *(adaṇḍena asatthena).* The use of relentless methods of punishment, including capital punishment, which were favored by the Brahmanical system,[12] are renounced. Such renunciation was also prompted by the Buddha's theory of knowledge, which did not allow for any absolute certainty regarding truth. Traditional Indian thought as well as the mainline Western philosophical tradition since Aristotle were committed to two truth values, the true and the false. This dichotomy also worked within the Western legal systems (see Chapter 15). The Buddha rejected this. Therefore, in the presence of an element of uncertainty regarding knowledge, the Buddha was not prepared to sacrifice even one single human life. The king is expected to follow a middle path between extreme severity and total laxity when adopting punitive measures. The relationship between the ruler and the ruled is comparable to one between a parent and child, where the parent acts with great compassion. In that context the purpose of punishment is correction, not revenge.

It was mentioned that the description of virtues was couched in the language of abstinence. However, in the presentation of the ideal monarch, they are presented in the form of commands: living beings ought not to be destroyed; what is not given ought not to be taken; wrongful indulgence in pleasures of sense ought not to be practiced; falsehood ought not to be spoken; spiritous liquor ought not to be drunk.[13] This problem will be discussed later in the context of law and morals (see Chapter 15).

The basic principles of the republican form of government, as mentioned earlier, were adopted by the Vajjians. The Vajjians were a prosperous *(mahiddhika)* and powerful *(mahānubhāva)* republic. As such, they earned the envy and wrath of the then king of Magadha, Ajātasattu. When the Buddha learned of the evil intention of Ajātasattu to destroy the Vajjians, he questioned Ānanda as to whether the Vajjians continued to observe the seven conditions listed below that would prevent the deterioration *(aparihāni)* of their republic.

1. Meeting regularly and frequently
2. Meeting in harmony, dispersing in harmony, and carrying on its business in harmony
3. Not authorizing what has not been authorized already, not abolishing what has already been authorized, but proceeding according to the ancient tradition
4. Honoring, respecting, revering, and saluting the elders and considering them worth listening to
5. Not forcibly abducting females and compelling them to live under a yoke
6. Honoring, respecting, revering, and saluting shrines at home and abroad without withdrawing offerings previously provided
7. Making appropriate provisions for the safety of the worthy ones *(arahats)* and the new arrivals, as well as those who are already present[14]

The first condition is intended to eliminate individualism in society. Isolating oneself from others is done on the assumption that one can be totally independent, an assumption that goes against the very grain of the Buddha's teaching, namely, dependent arising. Regular and frequent meetings tend to bring members of an organization together, provide them with an opportunity to understand each other, learn from each other, and help each other. Meeting in harmony and carrying on business in harmony, instead of adopting a hostile and competitive attitude, allow each person to make progress materially and morally while helping others achieve the same. Possessive individualism, which characterized the philosophies from Thomas Hobbes to John Locke and which has dominated social and political thinking in the modern Western world, was not part of the political philosophy of the Buddha.

The third condition may be taken as an attempt to preserve a status quo in social and political life and to not allow room for progress. On the contrary, it is a safeguard against total revolution. In the discussion on the status of the moral principle (see Chapter 10), I mentioned that revisions are most healthy when there is "maximum continuity and minimum jolt." Political change does not mean total and abrupt change, for this latter has proved to be harmful to the individuals involved. The wheel, as mentioned earlier, represents movement, but it is not the movement of a grasshopper. Respect for ancient wisdom is recommended. Elders in a society are the reservoirs of such wisdom, hence the need to honor and respect them.

The fifth condition is meant to preserve the dignity of the family. This micro-unit of the society is held together by the female. Mistreatment of the female thus is the most important condition leading to social and political decline.

Conditions six and seven are intended to preserve the moral fabric of the society. Objects of worship as well as the presence of morally perfect persons serve as a shield against evil and suffering, the elimination of which is the ultimate purpose of a political organization.

CHAPTER 15

Law, Justice, and Morals

THE FACT THAT the Buddha did not formulate in detail any definite laws for the guidance of the society is generally attributed to his lack of concern for this world and his emphasis upon otherworldly matters. The myth, perpetuated for a long time, that the Buddha was concerned primarily with otherworldly matters has been laid to rest by the research published in the last two decades dealing with the nature of early Buddhism by highly respected scholars,[1] as well as by my analysis of morals in this work. Because of his epistemology, if not for anything else, the Buddha was compelled to confine himself to this world. Yet, being in this world did not mean that the Buddha had to formulate laws for the governance of the people by a ruler or a group of representatives of the people, as did Kauṭilya. The Buddha was not setting up a charter for world government. He was more concerned with the welfare of human beings, not with a particular group of people, hence his formulation of the noble life as outlined earlier (see Chapters 6–9). The virtues and morals that constituted this noble life were therefore not presented as commands or laws but as things to be avoided *(veramaṇī)* or cultivated *(bhāvanā)*. What he expected was the ruler or rulers to follow these principles in formulating specific laws needed to govern a particular country, for he was aware that physical, geographical, as well as the historically evolved, cultural conditions were not the same everywhere in the world. His own concept of an ideal king, as explained in Chapter 14, was that of one who followed these principles. So he allowed the king to convert some of the basic virtues he inculcated into laws or commands. This is the very reason that the Universal Monarch is made to modify the descriptive language of the virtues from one of abstention to one of prohibition (see Chapter 14). It is the

Buddha's recognition that morals and laws have slightly differing purposes or goals. Thus, when the monks and nuns, who were committed to an ideal, came to live in communities of their own, the very same virtues had to be cast in the language of rules. Instead of appeal to abstinence, there is now prohibition. A wrong action is not proper *(akappiyaṃ)* and ought not be performed *(akaraṇīyaṃ)*.[2] This is the primary reason for calling rules of discipline *vinaya*, (*vi-naya*, lit., "leading in a different direction"; i.e., different from the normal course characterized by passion and hatred). This is the difference between virtues *(sīla)* and morals *(dhamma)* on the one hand and rules of discipline *(vinaya)* on the other.

While the conception of a Universal Monarch was presented as an ideal for any individual or community to adopt, the Buddha was directly involved in setting up an organization for his disciples. This organization came to be called the *saṅgha*, or "community," "group," "assembly," and so on (lit., *saṃ* + √*hr*, "to bring together"). The organization of this Community exemplifies the Buddha's conceptions of the individual and society (see Chapter 5) as well as his views regarding the nature and status of law.

Although the Community, or *saṅgha*, has been referred to as "a system of government formed by the Bhikkhus [monks] for the Bhikkhus and of the Bhikkhus"[3] and therefore a "democracy," it is more appropriately defined as a democratic institution set up by the Buddha for the good of its members as well as of humanity.

First, the Community was established as a means of providing the individual a training in the higher morality, in the cultivation of nobler mental attitudes through self-analysis and reflection, and in the development of wisdom. It was assumed that if a person were willing to renounce the household in order to achieve these ends, his or her commitment would be so great that the observance of the rules and precepts would not be a great obstacle.[4] In fact, the rules or laws were laid down with the intent to help the individual achieve his or her goal.

If the moral path is a middle path consisting of the avoidance *(vāritta)* of the extremes of self-indulgence and self-mortification, the most important feature of the monastic life would be the cultivation *(cāritta)* of contentment *(appicchatā)* until one attains ultimate freedom. It is therefore of interest to note that a good number of rules were formulated by the Buddha as a result of the indignation (described as *ujjhāyanti khī-*

yanti vipācenti) on the part of those who lived a life of contentment *(ye bhikkhu appicchā).*[5] The rules are thus meant to mold the character of the individuals who are part of the Community.

The Community has been criticized for its isolation from secular society. But this criticism is groundless even in the modern context. The Community is dependent on the laity for its material needs and in turn has the responsibility of educating the public, providing it with psychological and moral guidance. In other words, the Community carried the burden of creating a healthy-minded society. When the Community played such a vital role in the affairs of the society, it could not ignore public opinion. As a result, some of the rules were instituted because of the indignation of the people themselves *(manussā ujjhāyanti khīyanti vipācenti).*[6]

While the individual's welfare remained a major concern of the Community, the Community itself functioned with its own unity or identity, not simply as a group of unrelated individuals. The legislative, judiciary, and executive powers thus came to be vested in the Community. The four "great indicators" *(mahāpadesa)* explain the manner in which the laws came to be formulated. The four great indicators were taken to be valid if they were promulgated by the Buddha, by a unitary community, by a body of learned monks proficient in the laws *(vinayadhara),* and by a single learned monk proficient in the laws. Yet their validity had to be tested out by comparing them with and finding conformity in the existing body of doctrine and discipline *(dhamma-vinaya).*[7]

Juristic responsibilities are carried out by individual communities. However, they have to conform to the established body of rules or laws. Freedom to abandon the minor rules that have become outdated was already allowed by the Buddha.[8] The great indicators referred to above permitted the formulation of new rules in order to deal with new situations. The jurisdiction of each Community was limited by boundaries *(sīmā).*[9] In addition to the Community restricted by geographical "boundaries," there was the unified Community described as the "Community of the four quarters, of the present and the future" *(āgatānāgata cātuddisa saṅgha).*[10] The individual Communities become part of the collective Community through constant intercourse.

The subtle difference between morals and laws mentioned earlier appear once again in the manner in which the consequences of actions were experienced. In the sphere of morality, the consequences *(vipāka)* were dictated by a natural process of dependence. In the case of laws, the consequences were prescribed by the Community. The penal offenses were codified in terms of the gravity of the offense. Punishments were recommended accordingly. These punishments consisted of confessions; gating; asking for forgiveness; probation; deprivation of rights, privileges, and property; compulsory change of residence; public proclamation; social boycott; and expulsion. It is significant to note that the ultimate goal of all these forms of punishment was correction, not revenge. If one could not be corrected, the ultimate punishment was expulsion from the Community. In the societies in which these ideas prevailed, leaving the Community either on one's own initiative or as a result of banishment was considered so disgraceful that one lost any benefit gained from the society. It was not much different from the so-called "dishonorable discharge."

The reason a person receives such humane treatment under the Buddha's conception of law is best explained in the *Discourse to Prince Abhaya (Abhyayarājakumāra-sutta).*[11] Prince Abhaya, probably a follower of Jainism, urged by the Jaina leader Mahāvīra himself, went to debate the Buddha armed with a double-edged question *(ubhatokoṭikaṃ pañhaṃ).* Has the Buddha ever made a statement that would be disliked by and unpleasant to someone? Were the Buddha to respond in the positive, then he would be told that he was not different from an ordinary person. Were the Buddha to respond in the negative, then he would be reminded that he had indeed declared that Devadatta was doomed to a sorrowful way, to hell, would remain confined for an eon, and was incurable. Devadatta was certainly angry and displeased at these words. According to Mahāvīra, the Buddha would not be able to satisfactorily solve this puzzle. The question here is, Should one be unconditionally pleasant or unpleasant to others? Translating this into the language of penal laws, should one be pleasant to an evildoer and ignore his or her evil actions, or should one be unpleasant by imposing the most severe punishment, for no one likes punishment.

The Buddha had a surprise for Prince Abhaya. He referred to an innocent little baby boy lying on its back on Prince Abhaya's knees. The Buddha asked Prince Abhaya if this baby, through the prince's carelessness or that of his nurse, were to put a stick or a stone in his mouth, what would he (Prince Abhaya) do? Prince Abhaya's reply was that he would try to get the object out. If he failed the first time, he would take hold of the baby's head with the left hand and, crooking a finger, would get the object out with the right hand, even though it was covered with blood. When questioned by the Buddha as to why he should do so, Prince Abhaya's response was that he had compassion *(anukampā)* for the boy.

The Buddha then referred to six types of statements distinguished in terms of their truth value, utility, and emotive impact.

1. untrue[12]	useless	unpleasant
2. true[13]	useless	unpleasant
3. true	useful	unpleasant
4. untrue	useless	pleasant
5. true	useless	pleasant
6. true	useful	pleasant

The Buddha would only utter statements three and six, and that depending upon the appropriate time *(kālaññū),* not unconditionally. This means that pleasantness or unpleasantness are not criteria in determining whether an action of body or speech is right or wrong. Its truth value and usefulness, as well as the appropriateness of the time, are. Thus, if the Buddha were to say (or do) something unpleasant to another, he would do so as long as his statement (or action) were true, useful, and timely. This is because he had compassion for the beings *(sattesu anukampā).*

Concluding the discourse, the Buddha attributed his compassion to his understanding of the nature of the causal process *(dhammadhātu),*[14] which makes him treat each situation *(ṭhāna)* carefully, evaluating the conditions involved. This is an outright rejection of the belief in absolute and unconditional laws in favor of a concern for the human to whom punishments are meted out.

The above discussion of law and punishment would be incomplete without a reference to the conception of justice. Again the term for justice is *dhamma,* and its adjectival form, *dhammika,* is used to refer to whatever action that is "just." The conception of law and morals outlined above could not give rise to a standard of justice where positive law has to conform to "the immutable and unwritten laws of Heaven." The system of law worked out with great precision in the Western world is an inheritance of Graeco-Roman culture. Like its Indian and Islamic counterparts, it is based upon the celestial-terrestrial distinction. The Buddha's philosophy, as reiterated above, did not recognize such a distinction. Hence, his conception of justice has to remain at the terrestrial level. However, those who rejected transcendentalism and absolutism, and who wanted to present justice as a human phenomenon, argued that it is a mere convention, a human fabrication intended to keep the weak under control. Glaucon and Callicles, appearing in Plato's works, the *Republic*[15] and the *Gorgias*,[16] respectively, were classic representatives of this view. The Buddha, following a middle path, steered clear of these two extremes.

As a result of his confining himself to this world, the Buddha's conception of justice had to emerge from his understanding of the nature and status of both the individual and the society. We have already pointed out that according to him, the individual is a person with self-interest and the society represents "mutual self-interest." This definition of society includes the individual without sublating him or her. Accordingly, justice would be that which promotes mutual self-interest. A view similar to this has been presented in more recent times by John Rawls.[17] His view of justice as fairness is similar to that of the Buddha in that he places emphasis on human interest. According to Rawls, when a person becomes a part of a community, he or she is committed to recognizing common interests. A rational person therefore cannot expect others in the community to respect his or her interests unless he or she is prepared to respect the interests of others. This rationality is embodied in the Buddha's conception of a just act as one that leads to the welfare of oneself and others. Yet Rawls' theory of justice, even though it is a criticism of the utilitarian tradition, is heavily Kantian. In fact, he acknowledges this in the preface to his work.[18] We have already seen that the Buddha's conception of human freedom is very different from that of Kant in that it avoids the sort of absolute autonomy that the latter envisaged. Rawls' indebtedness to Kant, and his view that Kant's conception of autonomy is more important in his moral reflections than the notion of generality or universality,[19] stands in the way of comparing the Buddha's view of justice with that of Rawls. The Buddha's conception of freedom, as highlighted earlier (see Chapter 9), is less absolute and emphasizes the importance of another aspect absent in most Western conceptions of justice, namely, purity *(visuddhi)*. This combination of rationality and purity is clearly expressed in the Buddha's exhortation to his son, Rāhula.[20]

> If you, Rāhula, reflecting thus, should find, "That deed which I am desirous of doing with the body is a deed of my body that would conduce to the harm of self, to the harm of others, and to the harm of both, this deed of body is unwholesome, is productive of suffering, results in suffering,"—a deed of body like this, Rāhula, if indeed possible *(sasakkaṃ)*,[21] should not be done by you. [The statement is repeated with regard to deeds of speech and mind.]
>
> . . .
>
> But if you, Rāhula, while reflecting thus, should find, "That deed which I am desirous of doing with the body is a deed of my body that would conduce neither to the harm of self, nor to the harm of others, nor to the harm of both, this deed of body is wholesome, productive of happiness, results in happiness,"—a deed of body like this, Rāhula, may be done by you. [Repeated with regard to deeds of speech and mind.]

This explains the rationality discussed earlier. The Buddha then proceeds to give a further reason as follows:

> All those recluses and brahmans, Rāhula, who in the past purified *(parisodhesuṃ)* a deed of body, purified a deed of speech, purified a deed of mind, did so [only] after such repeated reflections. [Same with the present and future actions.]

Thus, justice as fairness is not for its own sake, but for the sake of purity and ultimate freedom.

CHAPTER 16

Nature and Morals

IN THE SPHERE of moral philosophy, as repeatedly emphasized in this work, the Buddha's clarion call was to adopt a way of life that leads to the welfare, happiness, and freedom both of oneself and others. He rejected deontology because it can call for self-sacrifice bordering on self-immolation. He renounced utilitarianism because it involves the majority-minority distinction wherein the minority may be called upon to suffer for the happiness of the majority. The Buddha's recommendation regarding the cultivation of the virtues of compassion *(anukampā)* and nonviolence *(ahiṃsā)* was unique in that it applied to both oneself and others. He differed from his contemporary, the Jaina Mahāvīra, in insisting that these virtues need to be practiced in relation to oneself as well. He agreed with Mahāvīra in extending their application to all living beings *(sabbabhūta)*, even though he did not adopt impractical measures to prevent unintentional injury. The practice of compassion and nonviolence is not something that can be forced or legislated. It has to come naturally, and this is the result of adopting a certain perspective about the nature of the world.

As explained earlier, the perspective in which the Buddha looked at the world can be summed up in one phrase: "dependent arising" *(paṭicca-samuppāda)*. Within this world of dependent arising there is another world that is the product of human dispositions *(saṅkhata)* (see Chapter 4), and it may be called the world of human culture. I have also argued that this world can appear in two forms: determined by human interest and dominated by greed. Culture determined by human interest emerges as a result of perceiving the world as being dependently arisen. Culture dominated by greed is the by-product of possessive individualism. When, in a recent publication,[1] the Venerable Dhammavihāri discussed nature as the cradle of human culture, he was contrasting the two forms of culture mentioned above and was attempting to show that what the Buddha and his disciples advocated was a culture of the first sort, which is closer to nature than the second, which is destructive to nature.

If the practice of compassion and nonviolence toward all living beings is to have any meaning, we need to recognize that nature or the natural environment belongs to all living beings, not merely humans. It would be inappropriate for human beings to assume that nature or the bounties of the natural environment are primarily for their consumption and enjoyment. The feeling that whatever there is in the natural environment is for the use of human beings arises as a result of the sharp distinction we make between humanity and nature, or our inability to perceive a close relationship between them.

The moral life explained earlier advocates the replacement of crude and unwholesome emotional tendencies with noble and wholesome ones. It encourages the elimination of selfishness and egoistic tendencies and the cultivation of nobler emotions such as the feelings of friendliness and compassion. When transforming one's personality in this manner, one does not have to totally abandon interest in oneself or others. In fact, without such interest the nobler emotions would be rendered lifeless. When greed and hatred are eliminated, when the dispositions are appeased, a human is able to understand his or her life as being dependently arisen in the same way the natural environment is conditioned. The Buddha's realization that all experienced phenomena are dependently arisen prevented him from recognizing a sharp dichotomy between humanity and nature. With that realization, nature does not appear either as something to be renounced for the sake of some higher mysterious spirituality or as something available primarily for the benefit of the humans. The principle of dependence provides a philosophical basis for relating oneself to the natural world. It allows for the development of a feeling of kinship with nature. The fervent hope on the part of Tālapuṭa, a disciple of the Buddha, is expressed in the following verse.

> When indeed could I evaluate dry wood, grass, the creepers and these aggregates [of mine] and the immeasurable mental capacities, these internal and external [worlds] as being equal *(sama)*? When could that [perspective] be mine?[2]

This feeling of kinship with nature is the basis of Buddhist culture. Culture is not confined to the production of great pieces of art and architecture. In fact, Buddhism was the forerunner in the production of some of the finest pieces of art and architecture in India. A more important part of culture is the manner in which we treat the surroundings in which we live. These surroundings include flora and fauna, rivers, lakes, forests, and mountains. Human beings, like other living beings, prefer to live in communities from which they derive their identities. Such community life calls for appropriate surroundings *(paṭirūpadesa).* People have lived in villages, transformed them into townships, and created cities. This in itself is not to be condemned. Culture is the refinement of one's way of living. Material conditions are a necessary component of it. The importance of material welfare in the life of human beings has already been pointed out. Unless that pursuit is not restrained by moral considerations, the appropriate surroundings could turn out to be the most inappropriate place for anyone to live. In this case, the difficulty lies in deciding when to draw the line between need and desire. It is here that rational human beings have to make a decision either individually or as a community. That rationality is often sublated by greed, selfishness, and possessive individualism, the elimination of which constituted the way as well as the conclusion of the moral life.

One place where nature exhibits life in its pristine purity as well as its mutual dependence is the natural forest *(jātavana).* The Indian ascetics in general, and the Buddha in particular, had great respect for the forest. Retirement into the forest had two specific goals. One was therapeutic, the other aesthetic.

It may be remembered that before his enlightenment the Buddha, after leaving the two contemplatives, Ālāra Kālāma and Uddaka Rāmaputta, and wandering around Magadha, arrived at a village called Uruvelā. There he found a delightful piece of land, a pleasant forest grove *(vanasaṇḍa),* with a river of clear water flowing by and surrounded by a village where he could go for alms *(gocaragāma).* He considered it an ideal place for a person desirous of striving *(padhānatthika).* He attained enlightenment and freedom here.[3] The therapeutic value of retiring to the forest is highlighted in a discourse delivered to a monk named Girimānanda.[4] At some point the Buddha was informed that Girimānanda had taken ill. Realizing that mental ill health can often lead to physical ailment, the Buddha advised Girimānanda to retire to a forest *(arañña)* or seek the shade of a tree *(rukkhamūla)* in order to develop the awareness *(saññā)* of impermanence *(anicca)*, nonsubstantiality *(anatta)*, impurity *(asubha)*, ill effect *(ādīnava)*, renunciation *(pahāṇa)*, passionlessness *(virāga)*, cessation *(nirodha)*, nondelight *(anabhirati)*, impermanence of all dispositions *(sabbasaṅkharesu anicca)*, and the awareness of breathing in and out *(ānāpānāsati)*. These ten forms of awareness pertain to the nature of the world as well as to oneself, an awareness that Tālapuṭa (a disciple of the Buddha, referred to earlier) was wishing for. The forest was the ideal environment for the development of such awareness not only because of the solitude it afforded, removed from the humdrum of urban life, the so-called world, but also because it certainly exhibited the characteristics of becoming, such as impermanence and nonsubstantiality. In that sense it is the best resort for one in need of psychological therapy. The Buddha took his son, Rāhula to this natural surrounding, a bamboo grove *(veḷuvana)* that was a feeding ground of the squirrels *(kalandakanivāpa)*, for instruction when he realized that the latter was ready for the attainment of enlightenment and freedom.[5] Remaining atop a mountain and having an aerial view of nature's beauty, a monk was able to tear asunder the veil of ignorance *(avijjā)* created by a world of artificiality.[6]

What is most interesting is that the natural forest, which provides a haven for someone desirous of overcoming the deadly defilements of greed, hatred, and confusion, also turns out to be a place of aesthetic enjoyment after the attainment of enlightenment and freedom. The earlier discussion on ethics should eliminate another long-standing myth about Buddhism: that a person attaining *nirvāṇa* is an otherworldly ascetic with no interest whatsoever in aesthetics. The elimination of greed, hatred, and confusion, which constitutes the attainment of enlightenment and freedom, has been understood as the total elimination of any and every form of human emotion. This view has been perpetuated in spite of Buddhism being the originator of art and architecture in the Indian subcontinent.

The monks often retreated into the forest "praised by the Buddha" *(buddhavaṇṇita)*[7] in order to enjoy its natural beauty. The charm of the forest is vividly described by many monks. One of them is Saṅkicca.

> Crags where clear waters lie, a rocky world,
> Haunted by black-faced apes and timid deer,
> Where cloaked in watery moss the rocks stand,
> Those are the highlands of my heart's delight.
> I've dwelt in forests and in mountain caves,
> In rocky gorges and haunts remote,
> And where the creatures of the wild do roam;[8]

Another monk saw harmony in experiences in the wild and the meditative culture he pursued.

> Fair-plumed, fair-crested passengers of air
> With deep and many hued wing,
> Give greetings to the muttering thunder cloud
> With cries melodious, manifold; 'tis they
> Will give thee joy whilst thou art musing there.[9]

Those who overcame the dangers arising from unmitigated pursuit of pleasures of sense were able to enjoy the forest habitat frequented by wild and ferocious beasts *(vāḷamiga)*,[10] even elephants in rut *(mattakuñjara)*.[11] The reason for their ability to survive in what appears to be hostile surroundings is the feeling of compassion and noninjury they emanated.

> I do not recollect any such evil wishes that these
> beings perish, that they be destroyed or that they
> suffer anguish and pain.[12]

Living amid nature's bounteous beauty, a monk was not prevented from either experiencing or expressing in the most artistic language a feeling of aesthetic pleasure.

> Clad with the azure bloom of flax, blue-flecked
> As sky in autumn; quick with crowds
> Of all their varied winged populace:
> Such are the braes wherein my soul delights.[13]

In addition to enjoying the natural forests, the Buddha also encouraged the grooming of new ones. Planting of trees was considered to be a good deed which brings about birth in heavenly worlds.[14] As mentioned earlier, the Buddha spent a good part of his life in a place called *Jetavanārāma* ("Jeta's forest grove"), the term for grove being *ārāma,* meaning "a place that delights the mind." Furthermore, to destroy a tree that has contributed much to the cleansing of the air that we breathe and has provided delightful shade during the hotter part of the day is looked upon as the betrayal of a friend *(mittadubbha).*[15] This sense of gratitude is symbolized in the legend about the Buddha's very first act after his attainment of enlightenment, when he stood gazing at the tree that gave him shade during his long struggle.

CHAPTER 17

Conclusion
The Stream and the Lotus Pond

THE FOREGOING description of the moral life and its ultimate goal is based upon what is considered the earliest corpus of Buddhist literature, leaving out those portions generally recognized as later additions even though they are included among the five collections *(nikāya or āgama)*. The first four collections, together with some of the books included in the fifth collection such as the *Sutta-nipāta, Udāna,* and *Itivuttaka,* or even the *Dhammapada,* in spite of the last being a redaction by the later Buddhists presented as a response to the *Bhagavadgītā,*[1] do not show any signs of a development of the doctrine indicative of an "early Buddha" and a "later Buddha," a distinction noticeable in the thoughts of some of the most respected systematic philosophers of the world. This of course does not prevent one from speaking of early Buddhism and later Buddhism. On the basis of the corpus of literature referred to above, it is possible to see that the statements of the Buddha, starting with the first discourse to the world, namely, *Said by the Tathāgata* (*Tathāgatena vutta,* or more popularly known as *The Discourse on the Setting of the Wheel of Righteousness, Dhammacakkappavattana-sutta*[2]) and concluding with his last words recorded in *the Discourse on the Great Decease (Mahāparinibbāna-suttanta),*[3] have one consistent philosophical standpoint characterized by a radical empiricism, a nonabsolutist metaphysics, and a pragmatic moral discourse. Depending upon the limited human knowledge and understanding provided by restrained sense experience and wisdom nourished by concentration, the Buddha formulated his principle of dependent arising. This principle of dependent arising, especially with its open-ended character, enabled the Buddha to explain human behavior, both moral and immoral, without resorting to any form of moral Absolute.

Two significant metaphors appear in these early discourses, one illustrating human life as it drifts along, conditioned by various factors such as the physical, psychological, and social, and the other signifying the behavior and status of a human being who has attained enlightenment and freedom. The first is the current, or flow, of a stream *(nadī-sota),* and the second is the lotus *(puṇḍarīka).* The two metaphors are related in a significant way, illustrating the subject matter of Chapters 6–9.

The flow of a stream can have many stages. First, it starts with the rain falling on high ground. As the water gradually accumulates and flows down to the lower level, it comes down cliffs and precipices, falls from one rock to another, and splashes all over. Next it flows smoothly on land with a gradual incline and no obstructions. All this time the stream is fed by various tributaries and is affected by other physical conditions. Finally, it can either join the great ocean and lose its identity or become arrested after reaching level land with no outlet. Here the water starts stagnating. It is only in this stagnant pond that the lotus plant grows; it does not grow in fast-flowing streams or in the salty ocean.

Human life, as understood by the Buddha, is a continuous process of becoming, of impermanence and change conditioned by various factors. This is called the stream of becoming *(bhavasota).*[4] While detailed and definite answers to questions such as, Did I exist in the past? Will I exist in the future?[5] were not attempted, the Buddha was willing to recognize the process of rebecoming[6] or rebirth *(jāti punappunaṃ)*[7] as one conditioned by a variety of factors.[8] This is comparable to the stream, which is itself conditioned by various factors, one of which is rainfall, unless of course we interpret the linguistic formulation of the activity of rain as "god sends down rain" *(devo vassati)*[9] rather literally.

Once life comes to be, it is conditioned, once again by a variety of factors. The process of learning begins. The "big blooming buzzing confusion" initially receives some ordering, thanks to the projenitors, who take care of the immediate needs. This is followed by an introduction to the world of knowledge accumulated by the society in which the person happens to be. In spite of that knowledge, a person is continually assailed by fear, uncertainty, and insecurity, and in these situations human thought functions like the stream tumbling over cliffs and precipices. It trembles, becomes unsteady *(phandanaṃ, capalaṃ)*, difficult to guard, and hard to check *(durakkhaṃ dunnivārayaṃ)*.[10] The discovery of the causes or conditions of such frightening situations, the possibility of overcoming them through an awareness of some form of regularity and uniformity, can bring about a measure of sanity. When this happens, once again thought starts flowing smoothly.[11] These are human conceptions based upon restrained human experience motivated by a desire to reduce anxiety and uncertainty.

Yet the worst of fears, namely, the fear of death, is not so easily overcome, unless one is strongly committed to the view that one will eventually attain immortality primarily on the basis of one's belief. The Buddha, who did not accept any such possibility, maintained that after death one can be reborn. Rebecoming is therefore comparable to the flow of the stream into the ocean, where it loses its temporary identity but provides a fertile ground for the generation of the clouds and rain that produce the stream. Remember that this is only a metaphor and can be interpreted in a rather absolutist way, as it happened in the later Buddhist tradition.

The Buddha, as well as those who followed him and attained enlightenment and freedom in this present life, has put an end to rebecoming. This is the inevitable consequence of the cessation of craving or the attainment of freedom. The Buddha and his followers are therefore referred to as those who "have terminated the stream" *(chinna-sota)*.[12] They do not return to the ocean.

What then are the conditions that produce a *buddha*, an enlightened one? We have referred to the two destinies of the stream: flowing into the ocean or becoming stagnant in land without an outlet. The society that produces a *buddha* is like the stagnant pond. Once the anxieties are reduced and the uncertainties are temporarily overcome, there is a tendency on the part of human beings to allow these conceptions to settle and become fossilized to such an extent that their flexibility is completely eliminated. We now have conceptions or theories that are supposed to be so true and real that the human beings who formulated them become hapless objects. They become the victims of the inexorable laws, the web that they themselves spun for their own security and welfare. This is what the Buddha called "the net of Brahma" *(brahmajāla)*, "the net of views" *(diṭṭhijāla)* (see Chapter 7). Caught up in this web of beliefs, human beings are ready to sacrifice their own kind for the sake of propagating or maintaining their belief systems. Conflicts and suffering in society are the inevitable outcome. Dogmatic adherence to views prevails, and compassion for human life or any form of life is absent.

This is human life turned into a stagnant pond. The flow or the flux is not there any more. Among the best plants that can survive in that stagnant pond is the lotus. It does not flourish in fast-flowing streams. Neither does it survive in the ever-churning salty oceans. It grows well in stagnant and dirty pools of water. The leaf as well as the flower of the lotus therefore develop a capacity to remain unsmeared by the water until the leaf rots or the flower that has risen above the water withers away.

The Buddha likened himself to a lotus born in the stagnant water of the world *(loke jāto)*, living in the stagnant water of the world *(loke ṭhito)*, yet remaining unsmeared by it *(lokena anupalitto)*.[13] A *buddha* appears when the wheel of righteousness, or the moral principle, has stopped rolling and is stuck in the muddy pond.

NOTES

Chapter 1: Pre-Buddhist Indian Moral Theories and Their Ultimate Developments

1. See S. Radhakrishnan, *Indian Philosophy,* vol. 1 (New York: The Macmillan Company; London: George Allen & Unwin, 1962), pp. 77f.
2. *Ṛgveda* 1.164.46.
3. *Bṛhadāraṇyaka* 1.4.1ff.
4. Ibid. 3.1.7ff.
5. *Ṛgveda* 1.164.20; *Muṇḍaka* 3.1.1; *Śvetāśvatara* 4.6.
6. *Bṛhadāraṇyaka* 1.4.11
7. *Ṛgveda* 10.90.
8. *Kena* 14–28.
9. *Bṛhadāraṇyaka* 3.6.
10. Radhakrishnan, *The Principal Upaniṣads,* pp. 168–169.
11. *Śvetāśvatara* 1.3,14.
12. *Bhagavadgītā* 2.39.
13. Ibid.
14. Ibid. 7.8–11.
15. Ibid. 18.40–44.
16. Ibid. 47.
17. Ibid. 66.
18. It is interesting that, while the Western deontologist Immanuel Kant rejected absolute self-sacrifice because for him the ultimate sanction for his conception of duty is "humanity," it is the utilitarian Mill who stated, "All honor to those who can abnegate for themselves the personal enjoyment of life when by such renunciation they contribute worthily to increase the amount of happiness in the world; but he who does it or professes to do it for any other purpose is no more deserving of admiration than the ascetic mounted on his pillar." See *Utilitarianism,* ed. George Sher (Indianapolis: Hackett Publishing Company, 1979), pp. 15–16.

19. *Ṛgveda* 10.190.
20. See statements in *Chāndogya* 8.15, 2.23; *Bṛhadāraṇyaka* 3.8.10.
21. *Jābala Upaniṣad* 4.
22. *Arthaśāstra,* p. 7.
23. *Bṛhadāraṇyaka* 1.4.11.
24. *Arthaśāstra,* p.5.
25. Ibid. p. 5.
26. Ibid. p.6.
27. *M* 1.482.
28. *Arthaśāstra,* p. 6.
29. Ibid. p. 8.
30. Ibid.
31. Ibid.
32. Ibid. p. 10.
33. Quoted in E. F. Schumacher, *The Small is Beautiful* (New York: Harper and Row, 1989), p. 24.
34. *Arthaśāstra,* pp. 6–7.
35. *D* 1.47–86.
36. Ibid. 1.55.
37. Ibid.
38. Barry Commoner, *Science & Survival* (New York: Ballantine Books, 1970), pp. 37–54.
39. Ibid.
40. Ibid.
41. *Dh* 39; also 412; *Sn* 520.
42. Ibid. p. 183.
43. *D* 1.56.
44. Ibid.
45. Ibid. 1.53.
46. Ibid. 1.54.
47. This was attempted by Udayana Ācārya in his *Nyāyakusumāñjali,* ed. Padmaprasada Upadhyaya, 2d. ed., pt. 1 (Benares: Chawkhambha Sanskrit Series Office, 1950), pp. 56–59.
48. *Vin* 1.71.
49. *HBP,* p. 16.
50. Ibid. pp. 17–18.
51. Quoted in Benimadhab Barua, *A History of Pre-Buddhistic Indian Philosophy* (Delhi: Motilal Banarsidass, 1970), p. 395.

Chapter 2: Knowledge

1. *M* 1.165–166.
2. Ibid. 1.167.

3. Ibid.
4. *S* 1.174.
5. Note the use of the term *vi-bhava,* instead of *a-bhava* (nonbecoming).
6. Ibid.
7. Ibid.
8. *D* 1.70.
9. Hilary Putnam, *Many Faces of Realism* (LaSalle, Illinois: Open Court, 1987), pp. 3–21.
10. *M* 1.136.
11. *HBP,* pp. 32–43.
12. William James, *The Principles of Psychology* (Cambridge, Mass.: Harvard University Press, 1983), pp. 573–574.
13. *S* 2.25.
14. *M* 2.171.
15. *S* 2.58.
16. *M* 1.395.
17. *A* 2.25.
18. *The Basic Works of Aristotle,* ed. Richard McKeon (New York: Random House, 1941), p. 1023.
19. Ibid.
20. Ibid. pp. 1024–1025.
21. Ibid. p. 1025.
22. David J. Kalupahana, *The Principles of Buddhist Psychology* (Albany: The State University of New York, 1987), pp. 28ff.

Chapter 3: The Fact-Value Distinction

1. *The Basic Works of Aristotle,* p.937.
2. Ibid.
3. *Principles of Buddhist Psychology.*
4. *M* 1.111–1.112.
5. *Sn* 916.
6. *S* 4.233.
7. *D* 3.105.
8. *S* 2.28ff.
9. *A* 2.79.
10. Ibid. 2.162.
11. *M* 1.65.
12. *S* 1.158, 200; 2.192; 4.216.
13. Ibid. 2.25.
14. *M* 1.167.
15. *S* 1.86; *Dh* 151, 168–169, 393.
16. *S* 2.17.

17. Saul A Kripke, "Identity and Necessity," in *Readings in Philosophical Psychology,* ed. Ned Block (Cambridge, Mass.: Harvard University Press, 1980), pp. 144–147.

Chapter 4: The World and the Will

1. *Principles of Buddhist Psychology,* p. 87.
2. Ludwig Wittgenstein, "A Lecture on Ethics" (1929–1930), *The Philosophical Review,* January 1965, pp. 3–12.
3. Incidentally, the Indian term for accidentalism before Buddha was *yadṛcchā.* The Buddha avoided the use of that term because in its Prakrit form—*yadicchā*—it could also mean "according to one's wish," a wish being something that he did not consider an accident, but one that is dependently arisen. Hence, he invented a new term, *adhiccasamuppāda,* meaning "arising on top of one another," with no connections or relations.
4. *S* 1.136; *A* 2.6.
5. *D* 1.53.
6. *M* 1.481; *S* 2.28,276; *A* 1.50; 4.190.
7. Ibid. 1.4–5.
8. *S* 3.87.
9. *HBP,* p. 75.
10. *S* 1.135.
11. Ibid. 2.43, 59.
12. Ibid. 2.37–41.
13. *A* 3.415.
14. *D* 2.99.
15. *M* 3.99–103.
16. *D* 3.217; *S* 2.82.
17. Karl R. Popper and John C. Eccles, *The Self and Its Brain* (New York: Springer International, 1985), pp. 38ff.
18. *D* 2.199.

Chapter 5: Individual and Society

1. *M* 1.135–136.
2. Ibid. 1.136.
3. *Śvetāśvatara* 1.14.
4. *S* 4.15; David J. Kalupahana, "Buddhist Tract on Empiricism," *Philosophy East and West* 19 (1969): 65–67; *Buddhist Philosophy. A Historical Analysis* (Honolulu: The University Press of Hawai'i, 1976), pp. 23–24.
5. *D* 1.202.
6. *M* 3.234–235.
7. *D* 3.80–98.
8. *S* 2.178.

9. Ibid. 3.86ff., *tad eva porāṇaṃ agaññaṃ akkharaṃ anupatanti, na tv ev' assa atthaṃ ājānanti.*
10. W. V. Quine, *Quiddities. An Intermittently Philosophical Dictionary* (Cambridge, Mass.: The Belknap Press of Harvard University Press, 1987), pp. 78, 111–114, 178, 186–189, 231.
11. *Bṛhadāraṇyaka,* 2.4.1–14.
12. *S* 1.75; *Ud* 47.
13. *M* 1.326ff.
14. Thomas Nagel, *The View From Nowhere* (New York, Oxford: Oxford University Press), 1986, p. 151.
15. *S* 3.30–31.
16. *A* 3.227.
17. *S* 3.31; also 2.173.
18. *D* 3.223.

Chapter 6: The Noble Life (*Brahmacariya*)

1. See A. B. Keith, *The Religion and Philosophy of the Vedas and the Upaniṣads* (Delhi: Motilal Banarsidass, 1970), 2.446ff.
2. *D* 2.251; also *M* 2.82.
3. *S* 5.6.
4. *D* 2.155; *M* 3.8.
5. *S* 5.2–3.
6. Ibid.
7. *D* 1.62.
8. *M* 1.514ff.
9. Ibid. 1.77.
10. *A* 3.227.
11. *M* 3.138–139.
12. *S* 2.19–20.
13. *M* 1.179.
14. Ibid. 1.179ff.
15. Ibid. 1.267ff.
16. *D* 2.251.
17. Ibid. 2.119–120.

Chapter 7: Virtues

1. *D* 1.1–46.
2. Ibid. 1.46.
3. See K. N. Jayatilleke, *Early Buddhist Theory of Knowledge* (London: George Allen and Unwin, 1963), pp. 1–168.
4. A 3.54.
5. *D* 1.12.
6. Ibid. 1.3, 12.

7. *A* 5.312.
8. *S* 1.13, 165.
9. *M* 2.27.
10. Ibid. 3.132.
11. Ibid. 3.136.
12. Ibid. 1.132.
13. Ibid. 2.51; see also 3.28–29.
14. *M* 3.132.
15. *A* 5.312, *kusalāni sīlāni anupubbena aggāya pārenti.*
16. *M* 1.80, 269, 346.
17. *S* 5.386–387.
18. *A* 4.246.
19. Ibid. 5.1–2.
20. Ibid.
21. Ibid. 2.98–99.
22. Ibid. 2.217.
23. *Saddharmapuṇḍarīka-sūtra* v.46.
24. *A* 1.226.
25. Ibid.4.220–222.

Chapter 8: The Eightfold Path

1. *M* 1.118.
2. Ibid. 1.167.
3. *S* 5.421.
4. *M* 3.71.
5. *HBP*, p. 103.
6. *M* 3.71–78.
7. *D* 2.312.
8. For a definition of the world, see Chapter 9.
9. *M* 3.234–235.
10. *D* 2.312.
11. Ibid. 2.313.
12. *A* 1.229.
13. *M* 3.289.
14. Ibid. 1.300–301; *S* 2.34.
15. *A* 4.203.
16. *S* 1.33; *Sn* 177.

Chapter 9: Freedom

1. *HBP*, pp. 90–100.
2. *Dh* 158.
3. *S* 5.5.

4. Ibid. 5.16.
5. *D* 3.84.
6. Ibid. 2.17.
7. *Dh* 174.
8. *A* 3.122, *dhammagaru tathāgato dhammagāravo.*
9. *Thag* 689.
10. *Vin* 1.35; *D* 1.84, 177, 203; *M* 2.39; *Sn* p.16.
11. *S* 1.122.
12. Ibid. 3.124.
13. *Thag* 625.
14. Ibid. 625, 722.
15. Ibid. 722.
16. Ibid. 830.
17. *Thig* 43–44, 69–70, 100, 103, 119, 124, 170, 178, etc.

Chapter 10: The Status of the Moral Principle

1. *Vin* 1.1.
2. Ibid. 1.2.
3. A vulture is said to be a symbol of greed and ruthlessness.
4. *M* 1.130.
5. See *HBP,* pp. 153–159.
6. *M* 1.134–135.
7. *HBP,* pp. 60–67.
8. See Asanga Tilakaratne, *Nirvana and Ineffability. A Study of the Buddhist Theory of Reality and Language* (Colombo, Sri Lanka: The Postgraduate Institute of Pali and Buddhist Studies, University of Kelaniya, 1993).
9. Ibid. 1.138.
10. See also *Causality. The Central Philosophy of Buddhism* (Honolulu: The University Press of Hawai'i, 1975), pp. 110–147. I have slightly modified the explanation given there.
11. *D* 2.12–15.
12. *S* 5.46.
13. *Thag* 303.
14. *A* 5.3–4. *Iti kho . . . dhammā 'va dhamme abhisandenti dhammā 'va dhamme paripūrenti apārā pāraṃ gamanāya.*
15. *M* 1.324.
16. William James, *Pragmatism,* ed. F. H. Burkhardt (Cambridge, Mass.: Harvard University Press, 1975), p. 35.
17. *D* 2.154, *Ākaṅkhamāno Ānanda saṅgho mam' accayena khuddānukhuddakāni sikkhāpadāni samūhantu.*
18. *Vin* 1.56,238.

Chapter 11: Justification of the Moral Life

1. *D* 3.234; *M* 1.73; *A* 4.459.
2. *A* 3.314.
3. *S* 1.228.
4. *A* 1.143–144.
5. Ibid. 1.142–143.
6. *D* 3.251.
7. *M* 2.194.
8. *D* 1.17; 3.29, *suññaṃ brahmavimānaṃ.*
9. *A* 1.127.
10. *It* 76–77.
11. *A* 1.141.
12. For a recent analysis of this ritual, see P. D. Premasiri, "Significance of the Ritual concerning Offerings to Ancestors in Theravada Buddhism," in *Buddhist Thought and Ritual,* ed. David J. Kalupahana (New York: Paragon House, 1991), pp.151–158.
13. *S* 4.206.
14. *M* 1.82; *S* 1.62; *A* 2.48; 4.429.
15. *M* 1.130.
16. *S* 2.19–20.
17. Ibid. 3.207–215.
18. Ibid. 3.209–210.
19. Ibid. 3.212.
20. Ibid. 2.97–105.
21. *A* 1.249.
22. *D* 1.196, 251; *M* 2.82.
23. See Ian Stevenson, *Cases of Reincarnation Type* (Charlottesville: University Press of Virginia, 1983).
24. *D* 1.82–83.
25. *S* 1.120–122.
26. Ibid. 3.119.
27. *D* 2.91–94.
28. *M* 1.266.
29. *D* 2.62–63.
30. Ibid.
31. See A. J. Ayer, *Concept of a Person and Other Essays* (London: Macmillan, 1963), p. 127.
32. See P. F. Strawson, *Individuals* (New York: Anchor Books, 1963).
33. *M* 1.258.
34. *Mūlamadhyamakakārikā* xvii.17.
35. *M* 1.400–413.

36. Ibid. 1.403.
37. Ibid. 3.169; *S* 5.455.
38. *Dh* 182.

Chapter 12: Society and Morals

1. *S* 1.99.
2. *M* 1.84–86.
3. Ibid. 2.128–129.
4. *Sn* 650.
5. *D* 3.84–96.
6. *Dialogues of the Buddha* (tr. of the *Dīgha-nikāya* by T. W. and C. A. F. Rhys Davids) (London: Pali Text Society, 1899–1921), 1.107.
7. *D* 3.75.
8. *A* 2.143.
9. *D* 3.180–193.
10. Ibid. 188–192; tr. by Maurice Walshe, *Thus Have I Heard. The Long Discourses of the Buddha* (London: Wisdom Publications, 1987), pp. 466–468.
11. *Sn* 149.
12. *M* 2.76ff.

Chapter 13: Economics and Morals

1. *View From Nowhere,* pp. 193ff.
2. *D* 3.58–79.
3. *Dh* 355.
4. Ibid. 155–156.
5. *A* 2.69–70.
6. *D* 3.154.
7. *S* 1.33.
8. Verses, 601–602, 1135–1136.
9. Ibid. 577.
10. E. F. Schumacher, *Small is Beautiful* (New York: Harper and Row, 1989), pp. 56–66.
11. *D* 3.155.

Chapter 14: Politics and Morals

1. *S* 4.374–380.
2. *D* 2.73–75.
3. Ibid. 2.76ff.
4. Ibid. 2.99–100.
5. Ibid. 3.58–79.
6. *S* 1.75–76.

7. Ibid. 5.423.
8. *D* 3.59.
9. *Sn* 260.
10. *D* 3.60.
11. Ibid. 3.61.
12. *Manusmṛti* vii.102.
13. *D* 2.62.
14. Ibid. 2.73–75.

Chapter 15: Law, Justice, and Morals

1. K. N. Jayatilleke was one of the first to undertake a detailed analysis of the early Buddhist theory of knowledge. In spite of his belief that ultimate freedom is transcendental in the sense of being "beyond the world," Jayatilleke's analysis of human knowledge opened the door to a non-transcendentalist interpretation of Buddhism. See his *Early Buddhist Theory of Knowledge.* See especially his work on "The Principles of International Law in the Buddhist Doctrine" in *Recueil des Cours* vol. 2 (Leiden, Holland: A. W. Sijthoff, 1967), pp. 445–563.
2. *Vin* 1.59, 211, 216, 250, 305; 2.2, 7, 8, 73; 3.20, 22, 42.
3. G. De, *Democracy in Early Buddhist Sangha* (Calcutta: Calcutta University, 1955), p. xv.
4. *A* 1.230.
5. *Vin* 1.53, 58, 60–62, 102, etc.
6. Ibid. 1.43, 74–75; 3.72, etc.
7. *D* 2.123–125.
8. Ibid. 2.154.
9. See Ariyasena Thera, "Early Buddhist Bhiksu Organization," quoted in Jayatilleke, *Recueil des Cours,* p. 521.
10. *Vin* 2.147.
11. *M* 1.392–396.
12. *HBP,* pp. 51–52.
13. Ibid.
14. Compare *S* 2.25–26.
15. *Plato: Collected Dialogues,* ed. Edith Hamilton and Huntington Cairns (New York: Bollingen Foundation, 1961), pp. 605–607.
16. Ibid. pp. 265–267.
17. John Rawls, *A Theory of Justice* (Cambridge, Mass.: Harvard University Press, 1971).
18. Ibid. p. 8.
19. Ibid. pp. 251–252.
20. *M* 1.414–1.420.
21. It is interesting to note that this term is taken by the commentarial tradition to mean "surely, certainly, definitely"; i.e., as a synonym for *ekam-*

sena, Papañcasūdanī, Majjhimanikāya-aṭṭhakathā (PTS), 3.128. Such an interpretation would not be very compatible with the function of morals in the early discourses discussed in the earlier part of this chapter. Interestingly, the editors of the Pali Text Society's *Pali-English Dictionary* do not follow the commentary.

Chapter 16: Nature and Morals

1. Ven Dhammavihari, *A Correct Vision and A Life Sublime* (Kolonnawa, Sri Lanka: Lanka Printing, 1990), pp. 9–16. This small volume contains a set of extremely poignant essays by the former Prof. J. D. Dhirasekera published on the occasion of his higher ordination.
2. *Thag* 1101.
3. *M* 1.166–167.
4. *A* 5.108–112.
5. *M* 3.477.
6. *Thag* 544.
7. Ibid. 537.
8. Ibid. 601–602; *Psalms of the Early Buddhists,* tr. by C. A. F. Rhys Davids (London: Pali Text Society, 1903–1913).
9. *Psalms of the Early Buddhists,* p. 1136.
10. Ibid., p. 602.
11. Ibid., p. 539.
12. Ibid., p. 603.
13. Ibid., p. 1068.
14. *S* 1.33.
15. *Pv* 259.

Chapter 17: Conclusion

1. See David J. Kalupahana, *A Path of Righteousness (The Dhammapada)* (Lanham, Maryland: The University Press of America, 1986), pp. 54–62.
2. *S* 5.420–424.
3. *D* 2.151.
4. *S* 1.15, 4.128.
5. Ibid. 3.94–99.
6. *D* 2.15; *S* 1.133.
7. *Dh* 153; *Thag* 183, 255.
8. *M* 1.265.
9. *D* 1.74.
10. *Dh* 33.
11. William James, *The Will to Believe,* ed. F. Burkhardt (Cambridge, Mass.: Harvard University Press, 1976), pp. 58–59.
12. *Sn* 1034; *S* 4.292.
13. A 2.38–39; *Thag* 700–701.

GLOSSARY
The Technical Vocabulary

TECHNICAL TERMS occurring in Western discussions of ethical theory had to be used in the present explanation of the Buddha's views on ethics. This would not be problematic if the early Buddhist theory were to be identical with any one of the major ethical theories in the Western world, for that would enable the Western reader familiar with the different theories to place him- or herself in any one of these positions to try to understand that standpoint in relation to the opposing theories. However, this is not possible, for it is difficult to find any one philosophical system with which early Buddhism may appear to be in agreement in regard to every conception or theory. As I have tried to explain here as well as in my other publications, the one system that comes anywhere close to sharing a majority of philosophical ideas with early Buddhism is Jamesean pragmatism. Yet that does not mean they are identical. For example, while the Buddha was willing to apply his theory of nonsubstantiality even to the goal of the moral life, namely, *nibbāna,* and thereby maintain a relationship between the moral life and its ultimate goal, James insisted on making a sharp distinction between the moral life and the religious life, the latter being associated with a form of "spirituality" that James found mystical and that is shared by all the major religious leaders as well as by a large number of ordinary people who claimed to have visions, which are not easily verifiable. The vision the Buddha spoke of was not of something unverifiable.

For this reason, it was thought that a few of the major technical terms used in ethical discourse should be examined, indicating briefly their applicability (or inapplicability) to the doctrine of the Buddha.

Absolute. A moral Absolute is defined as a principle that is universally binding, not only because it applies to all people at all times under any circumstances, but also because it can never be overriden by any other principle. For epistemological, ontological, ethical, and linguistic reasons discussed in this work, the Buddha could not subscribe to such a moral Absolute.

Altruism. This is generally explained as unselfish regard or concern for others or disinterested other-regarding action. For the Buddha, there was no single definition of the selfish or the disinterested. As highlighted in this work, self-interest can vary from the most rudimentary, which is natural, to the most extreme and compounded, such as greed, avarice, craving, or lust, which are unnatural and abominable. If by altruism we mean consciously and knowingly destroying one's own life for the sake of others, the Buddha would have had difficulty accepting it. Compassion for others is not something that should override compassion for oneself. Here again, without being an absolutist or without rationally posing dilemmas that would entail the destruction of oneself for the sake of others, the Buddha would attempt to find a middle ground that would lead to the happiness of oneself and others.

Autonomy. Derived from the Greek term *nomos,* "order," it can literally mean "one's own order," which, in the most general sense, implies independence. In modern Western philosophy, it was Kant who emphasized this idea, using it as a technical term by contrasting it with heteronomy, "other order." It was pointed out that the strict boundaries or demarcations that gave rise to two contrasting phenomena, namely, self and other, were dismissed by the Buddha on the basis of the principle of dependence. The conception of absolute independence, not recognized in the early discourses, hence without a technical term to refer to it, was subsequently mentioned by Nāgārjuna. However, he had to utilize the term *apratītyasamutpanna,* which is the negation of the central conception of the Buddha, namely, *pratītyasamutpanna.* Nāgārjuna, of course, denied that there could be anything like it.

Deontology. This term is derived from the Greek *deon,* "duty" or "obligation." Deontological ethical theories vary depending upon where the notion of duty or obligation is anchored. In the theistic systems, deontological theory is established on God's will. In the nontheistic absolutist traditions, such as the early *Upaniṣads,* it is related to the ultimate moral absolute that generated the fourfold caste system. In the more recent Kantian system, it is pegged onto humanity and its autonomy. In the early Buddhist context, the term that can come close to the the idea of duty or obligation is *karaṇīyaṃ,* "ought to be done." However, it does not express the stronger notion of "duty for duty's sake" or the "intrinsic value of the moral act," for what "ought to be done" is not determined by one single condition, but a whole variety of conditions.

Emotivism. This is a product of the theory of noncognitivism in ethics, which upholds the view that values, in contrast to facts that are cognitive, are mere attitudes. It can be defined as a form of amoralism. However, the proponents of the theory are not immoral persons, but only those who have difficulty speaking philosophically about morals. The elimination of the sharp dichotomy between facts and values in the Buddha's doctrine prevents it from being either a form of emotivism or positivism in which these traditions are generally defined.

Pragmatism. It was stated that if there is any "ism" that can be compared with Buddhism, it would be pragmatism with a moral foundation. However, the moral pragmatism growing out of the Christian background in America still retains some aspects of Christian spiritualism, that is, the belief in a power higher than the power of the mortals, and this has given rise to the distinction between the moral and the religious, a distinction that is not observable at least in the early Buddhist tradition.

Utilitarianism. This, of course, is the most popular ethical theory in the modern world, next to theistic deontology. It has two versions. One reaches back to Jeremy Bentham and advocated maximum pleasure as the criterion for determining what is good, and even provided a hedonic calculus by which one could measure the maximum pleasure. The second version is the more enlightened form proposed by J. S. Mill, who argued for maximum happiness. Human happiness is also a criterion for determining what is right and wrong in the Buddhist tradition. However, in utilitarianism, the maximum is calculated not only in terms of maximum happiness, but also in relation to the number of people who can enjoy it. Thus, we have the distinction between the majority and the minority. Utilitarianism thus provided a foundation for the sacrifice of the individual for the sake of the larger entity, the society, an idea not encouraged in the Kantian deontology with its emphasis on humanity. Deontology of the theological traditions, of course, advocated the sacrifice of the individual. Early Buddhism differs from utilitarianism in that it, while speaking of the welfare and happiness of the many, inculcates compassion for the whole world. This means that no individual is to be sacrificed for the sake of the many. So, the criterion does not entail the majority/minority distinction, but proposes a way to discover a "genuine good" *(sadattha)* that would involve the welfare and happiness of both oneself and others.

SELECT BIBLIOGRAPHY

Primary Sources

Aṅguttara-nikāya. Ed. R. Morris and E. Hardy. 5 vols. London: Pali Text Society, 1885–1900; Woodward, F. L., and E. M. Hare, trans. *The Book of the Gradual Sayings.* 5 vols. London: Pali Text Society, 1932–1936.

Aṅguttara-nikāya-aṭṭhakathā, Manorathapūraṇī. Ed. M. Walleser and H. Kopp. 5 vols. London: Pali Text Society, 1924–1956.

Arthaśāstra of Kauṭilya. Ed. with commentary by T. G. Sastri. 3 vols. Trivandrum: Oriental Library, 1912–1925; Shamasastri, R., trans. *Kauṭilya's Arthaśāstra.* 4th ed. Mysore, India: Sri Raghuveer Printing Press, 1951.

Bhagavadgītā. Text and trans. Winthrop Sargent. Rev. by Christopher Chapple. Albany: State University of New York, 1984.

Dhammapada. Ed. S. Sumangala Thera. London: Pali Text Society, 1914; Kalupahana, David J., ed. and trans. *A Path of Righteousness.* Lanham, Md.: The University Press of America, 1986.

Dīgha-nikāya. Ed. T. W. Rhys Davids and J. E. Carpenter. 3 vols. London: Pali Text Society, 1890–1911.

Itivuttaka. Ed. E. Windish. London: Pali Text Society, 1889.

Majjhima-nikāya. Ed. V. Trenckner and R. Chalmers. 3 vols. London: Pali Text Society, 1948–1951; Horner, I. B., trans. *The Middle Length Sayings.* 3 vols. London: Pali Text Society, 1954–1959.

Petavatthu-aṭṭhakathā. Ed. J. Minayeff. London: Pali Text Society, 1888.

Pratītyasamutpāda-sūtra. Ed. N. P. Chakravarti, 179–199. Vol. 21 of *Epigraphia Indica.* Delhi: Government of India, 1931.

Ṛgveda. See *Ṛgvedasaṃhitā.* Ed. F. Max Muller. 6 vols. London: W. H. Allen, 1849–1874; Muller, F. Max, trans. *Vedic Hymns: The Sacred Books of the East.* Vol. 32. Oxford: The Clarendon Press, 1891; Maurer, Walter H., trans. *Pinnacles of India's Past: Selections from the Ṛgveda.* Amsterdam and Philadelphia: John Benjamins Publishing Company, 1986.

Saṃyutta-nikāya. Ed. L. Feer. 6 vols. London: Pali Text Society, 1884–1904.

Śathapatha Brāhmaṇa. Ed. V. S. Gauda, C. Sharma, and S. V. Sastri. 2 vols. Benares, India: Acyuta Granthamala Karyalaya, 1922–1937.
Sutta-nipāta. Ed. D. Anderson and H. Smith. London: Pali Text Society, 1913.
Sutta-nipāta-aṭṭhakathā. Ed. H. Smith. 2 vols. London: Pali Text Society, 1916–1917.
Sūyagadam (Sūtrakṛtāṅga). With commentary of Silanka. Ed. A. S. Suri and C. Ganindra. 2 vols. Bhavanagara, Bombay: Vijayadeva Sura, 1950–1953.
Theragāthā. See *Thera-therī-gāthā.* Ed. H. Oldenberg and R. Pischel. London: Pali Text Society, 1883.
Therīgāthā. See *Theragāthā.*
Taittiriya Brāhmaṇa. Ed. Rajendralal Mitra. *Bibliotheca Indica.* 3 vols. Calcutta: Asiatic Society of Bengal, 1859.
Udāna. Ed. P. Steinthal. London: Pali Text Society, 1948.
Upaniṣads. See *The Principal Upaniṣads.* Ed. and trans. S. Radhakrishnan. London: George Allen & Unwin, 1953; Hume, R. E., trans. *The Thirteen Principal Upaniṣads.* London, Oxford, and New York: Oxford University Press, 1971.
Vibhaṅga. Ed. C. A. F. Rhys Davids. London: Pali Text Society, 1904.

Secondary Sources

Ayer, A. J. *Concept of a Person and Other Essays.* London: Macmillan, 1963.
Barua, Benimadhab. *A History of Pre-Buddhistic Indian Philosophy.* Delhi: Motilal Banarsidass, 1970.
Commoner, Barry. *Science and Survival.* New York: Ballantine Books, 1970.
De, G. *Democracy in Early Buddhist Sangha.* Calcutta: Calcutta University Press, 1955.
Dharmasiri, Gunapala. *Fundamentals of Buddhist Ethics.* Antioch, Calif.: Golden Leaves Publishing Company, 1989.
Dhammavihari, Venerable. *A Correct Vision and a Life Sublime.* Kolonnawa, Sri Lanka: Lanka Printing, 1990.
Hamilton, Edith, and Huntington Cairns, eds. *Plato: Collected Dialogues.* New York: Bolingen Foundation, 1961.
James, William. *Pragmatism.* Ed. F. Burkhardt. Cambridge, Mass.: Harvard University Press, 1975.
———. *The Will to Believe.* Ed. F. Burkhardt. Cambridge, Mass.: Harvard University Press, 1979.
———. *The Principles of Psychology.* Ed. F. Burkhardt. Cambridge, Mass.: Harvard University Press, 1983.
Jayatilleke, K. N. *Early Buddhist Theory of Knowledge.* London: George Allen & Unwin, 1963.

———. "The Principles of International Law in Buddhist Doctrine." In *Recueil des Cours*. Vol. 2. Leiden, Holland: A. W. Sijthoff, 1967.

Kalupahana, David J. *Causality: The Central Philosophy of Buddhism*. Honolulu: The University Press of Hawai'i, 1975.

———. *Buddhist Philosophy: A Historical Analysis*. Honolulu: The University Press of Hawai'i, 1976.

———. *The Principles of Buddhist Psychology*. Albany, N.Y.: The State University of New York Press, 1987.

———. *A History of Buddhist Philosophy*. Honolulu: University of Hawai'i Press, 1992.

———. "Buddhist Tract on Empiricism." In *Philosophy East and West* 19 (1969): 65–67.

———, ed. *Buddhist Thought and Ritual*. New York: Paragon House, 1991.

Kant, Immanuel. *Foundations of the Metaphysics of Morals*. Trans. Lewis White Beck; text and critical essays ed. Robert Paul Wolff. New York: Macmillan Publishing Company, 1984.

Keith, Arthur B. *The Religion and Philosophy of the Vedas and the Upanisads*. Delhi: Motilal Banarsidass, 1970.

Kripke, Saul A. "Identity and Necessity." In *Readings in Philosophical Psychology*. Ed. Ned Block, 144–147. Cambridge, Mass.: Harvard University Press, 1980.

McKeon, Richard. *The Basic Works of Aristotle*. New York: Random House, 1941.

Mill, John Stewart. *Utilitarianism*. Ed. George Sher. Indianapolis: Hackett Publishing Company, 1979.

Nagel, Thomas. *The View from Nowhere*. New York and Oxford: Oxford University Press, 1986.

Pojman, Louis P. *Ethics: Discovering Right and Wrong*. Belmont, Calif.: Wadsworth Publishing Company, 1990.

Popper, Karl R., and John C. Eccles. *The Self and Its Brain*. New York: Springer International, 1985.

Premasiri, P. D. *Ethics*. Reprinted from *Encyclopaedia of Buddhism*. Colombo, Sri Lanka: Department of Buddhist Affairs, 1991.

Putnam, Hilary. *The Many Faces of Realism*. LaSalle, Ill.: Open Court, 1987.

Quine, W. V. *Quiddities: An Intermittantly Philosophical Dictionary*. Cambridge, Mass.: The Belknap Press, 1987.

Radhakrishnan, S. *Indian Philosophy*. Vol. 1. New York: The Macmillan Company; London: George Allen & Unwin, 1962.

Rawls, John. *A Theory of Justice*. Cambridge, Mass.: Harvard University Press, 1961.

Saddhatissa, H. *Buddhist Ethics*. New York: George Braziller, 1971.

Schumacher, E. F. *The Small is Beautiful*. New York: Harper and Row, 1989.

Sher, George, ed. *Utilitarianism.* Indianapolis: Hackett Publishing Company, 1979.

Stevenson, Ian. *Cases of the Reincarnation Type.* Charlottesville: University Press of Virginia, 1983.

Strawson, P. F. *Individuals.* New York: Anchor Books, 1963.

Tilakaratne, Asanga. *Nirvana and Ineffability: A Study of the Buddhist Theory of Reality and Language.* Colombo, Sri Lanka: The Postgraduate Institute of Pali and Buddhist Studies, University of Kelaniya, 1993.

Wittgenstein, Ludwig. "A Lecture on Ethics." (1929–1930). *The Philosophical Review* (January 1965): 3–12.

INDEX

a priori, 13, 29, 32, 33
Absolute, 35; moral 5, 47, 60, 65, 71, 88, 106, 144; nondual, 54, 84
absolutism, 71, 135; non-, 21, 33
abstinence, 15, 80, 128, 131
action (karma, *kamma*), 13, 51; *(kiriya)*, 19, 21–24; deterministic theory of, 100–101; doctrine of, 14, 60, 71, 99, 106–108, 120; fruits or consequences of, 8, 9, 12, 107; previous, 113, 126
accidentalism *(addhiccasamuppāda)*, 48, 67; accidental *(adhiccasamuppanna)*, 57, 100
aesthetic(s), 13, 35, 37, 39, 40, 139–141
afterlife, 107, 108
Ajita Kesakambali, 16–19, 79, 106, 107
Ājīvikas, 19, 21
Ālāra Kālāma, 28, 139
amoralism, 16, 18–21, 48
Ānanda, 66, 70, 104, 128
annihilation *(uccheda)*, 8, 86
anomalous, 3
anxiety *(paritassanā)*, 31, 54, 93, 145
Aristotle (Aristotelean), 34, 35, 38, 39, 72, 127
art, 35, 53, 139–140
Āryan, 10, 12, 115
ascetic *(śramaṇa, samaṇa)* tradition, 10, 16, 20–23, 45, 49, 91, 106, 120; asceticism, 10, 26, 35, 50
Aśoka (Emperor), 16, 126
attachment *(ālaya)*, 29; *(rāga)*, 30, 60, 67, 97, 121
austerity *(tapas)*, 24, 67
autonomy, 29, 48, 135
aversion *(dveṣa, dosa)*, 30, 67, 90, 97
avoidance, 40, 73, 78, 131

becoming *(bhava)*, 42, 79, 83, 96, 97, 100, 103, 140; craving *(taṇhā)* for, 28; stream *(-sota)* of, 144
Bentham, Jeremy, 13
Bhagavadgītā, 6–10, 12, 13, 15, 47, 100, 124, 143
birth *(jāti)*, 11, 17, 20, 28, 97, 101, 105, 113, 126, 127, 141; spontaneous, 108; rarity of, 108
brahma (the moral Absolute), 4–7, 9, 11, 21, 32, 37, 40, 54, 56, 60, 70, 94; union with, 97
Brahmā (god), 60, 71, 72, 145
Brahmanism, 10, 20, 21, 25

capitalist, 15
caste *(varṇa)*, 5, 6, 8, 11, 12, 15, 21, 44, 56, 60, 67, 77, 85, 97, 113, 120, 124, 125

celestial, 3, 4, 6, 16, 20, 24, 28, 35, 39, 71, 135
certainty, 21, 37, 82, 100, 127
cessation *(nirodha)*, 29; of birth, 97, 140; of causes *(paccaya)*, 86, 90; of craving *(taṇhā)*, 145; of perception and what is felt *(saññāvedayita)*, 30; of the world *(loka)*, 99
change, 115, 144; constant, 83; and disappearance, 86; empirical world of, 27; grammatical, 41; identity without, 28; (linguistic), 56; movement and, 126; not subject to, 54; world of, 88
clairvoyance *(dibbacakkhu)*, 101, 103, 104, 106
Commoner, Barry, 17
communism, 121
Comte, Auguste, 38
conception *(paññatti, saṃkappa, saṅkhā)*, 43, 56, 57, 66, 121; right *(sammā)*, 77, 79–82; conceptual, 66, 121; -apparatus, 32, 66; -order, 43; -world, 81
conditionality *(idappaccayatā)*, 29, 31, 67, 94, 95, 103, 106
confession, 94
confidence *(saddhā)*, 50, 90, 97; reasonable *(ākāravatī)*, 106
conflicts *(raṇa)*, 55, 56, 146
confusion *(musā)*, 33, 34, 86, 87, 97, 140; big blooming buzzing, 144
consciousness *(viññāṇa)*, 40–43, 50, 51, 53, 93, 99, 104, 105; stream of *(sota)*, 41, 42
contact *(phassa)*, 40, 41, 43
contentment, 131, 132
correction, 128, 133
craving *(taṇhā)*, 28, 29, 59, 79, 104, 122, 145
death *(maraṇa)*, 28, 97, 98; after, 107, 108; by fasting, 24; fear of, 75, 145; moment of, 88, 101, 105; one-life-after-, 104; pangs of, 52
deductive reasoning *(takka)*, 27, 32, 33, 91; method, 13; search, 37
demerit *(pāpa)*, 18, 53
democracy, 131
departed spirits *(peta)*, 96, 98, 99
dependence, 42, 50; language of, 32, 43; mutual, 139; natural process of, 133; principle of, 41, 90, 93, 94, 138
dependent arising *(paṭiccasamuppāda)*, 29, 31, 33, 44, 48, 67, 84, 87, 90, 93–95, 103, 104, 114, 129, 137, 143
dependently arisen *(paṭicasamuppanna)*, 43, 44, 51, 137, 138
Descartes, Rene, 22
determinism, 23, 24, 95, 102; biological, 16, 19, 21; determinists, 50
Devadatta, 133
dharma *(dhamma)*, conditions, 99; doctrine, 132; enlightened one not above, 87; events, 33; fact and value, 43–44; good, 114; ideas, 81; justice, 134; law-likeness, 94; moral principle, 44, 94; morals, 36, 65, 70, 72, 74, 93, 131; naturalness *(dhammatā)*, 75, 93; phenomena, 49, 82; righteous *(dhammika)*, 127; statement and content of doctrine, 92
Dignāga, 56, 105
dispositions *(saṅkhāra)*, 42, 49–53, 59, 80, 92, 121, 137, 138, 140; appeasement *(upasama)*, 29, 42, 59; dispositionally conditioned *(saṅkhata)*, 48, 82, 137; types of, 51, 53
divine, 9, 12, 98, 126
duty, 6, 8, 9, 15, 65, 124

effort *(viriya)*, 20, 21, 23, 24, 45, 49, 50, 107
empiricism, 13, 31–33, 39, 78, 113, 143
enlightenment, 29, 42, 50, 53, 66–69, 71, 72, 77, 83–90, 102, 103, 126, 139, 140, 142, 144, 145
environment, 61, 120, 123, 138, 140
epistemology, 12, 13, 22, 24, 27, 33–35, 39, 78, 91, 92, 130
etymology *(nirukti)*, 55, 56
evolution, biological, 100; of the world and society, 114, 115, 126; of the world process, 57, 86

friendliness *(mettā)*, 61, 97, 118, 138

Glaucon, 60, 119, 135
God, 20, 60, 100, 108
gods *(deva)*, 3–7, 11, 15, 17, 58, 71, 96, 97, 109
grammar *(vyākaraṇa)*, 55, 56
grasping *(upādāna, abhinivesa)*, 29, 45, 53, 79, 92
greed, 14, 15, 59, 60, 87, 115, 121, 122, 137–140
Greeks, 38

health, 26, 99, 140
heaven *(sagga)*, 66, 87, 97, 101, 117, 134
hedonic, 13, 74
hell *(niraya)*, 98, 101, 102, 107, 108, 133
horizon, 42, 74
humanity, 7, 9, 47, 131, 138

idealist, 42
identity, 54, 144, 145; of *atma* and *brahma*, 5; of the Community, 132; concept of, 66; criterion for, 105; of the human personality, 51
impermanence *(anicca)*, 27, 30, 41, 45, 95, 108, 140, 144
impurity, 19, 20, 140
incorruptible, 27, 35, 39, 44; (concepts), 43, 66; incorruptibility, 27, 39, 42; law, 82, 94; universals, 56
independence, 29
indignation, 131, 132
individualism, 87, 129; possessive, 78, 137, 139
inductive reasoning, 33, 78
ineffability, 32, 34, 92
inference, 33, 91
inner controller *(antaryāmin)*, 5, 93
intelligence, 8, 102, 109
intention, 22, 121
interest, 42, 59–61, 83, 121, 137, 138; mutual self-interest, 114, 115; self-interest, 119
intuition, 55; non-conceptual, 121; non-sensuous, 14, 29, 54; transcendent, 31; yogic 7, 13, 32, 72

Jainism, 16, 20, 21, 24, 25, 85, 133
James, William, 31, 39, 43

Kant, Immanuel, 39, 47, 48, 50, 135
Kantian, 29, 30, 39, 135
karma, 14, 60, 71, 99–101, 106–108, 120; deterministic theory of, 100–101; past, 113, 126
Kauṭilya, 12–16, 130
Keynes, Lord, 15

language, absolute laws in, 90; of abstinence, 128; artistic, 141; Buddha's terms for, 56; conception and, 79, 80, 82; of dependence, 32, 43, 104; fluidity of, 55; language drift, 57; like a raft, 92; mirror of reality, 55; non-absolutist use of, 57; not expressible

in, 48; passive, 41; of penal laws, 133; of prohibition, 130; of rules, 131; ultimate constituents of, 55
laws, 130, 134; absolute, 3, 10, 44, 90, 145; eternal, 126; invariable, 72; moral, 34, 38, 91; morals and, 130–131; penal, 133; physical, 17; proficient in, 132; of punishment, 14
limitations, 67, 79
limits, 42, 48, 61, 66
logic, 32–35, 38, 39, 72

Mahāvīra, 20–24, 26, 27, 32, 95, 133, 137
Mahāyāna, 84, 87
materialism, 16–18, 119
materialistic, 13, 120
materialists, 7, 27, 71
meaningless, 35, 36, 38, 80, 102
memory *(sati)*, 41, 103–106
merit *(puñña)*, 18, 53, 79, 98
metaphysics, 18, 22, 24, 27, 35, 39, 47, 65, 100, 107, 142
middle path *(majjhimā paṭipadā)*, 45, 55, 56, 58, 80, 87, 99, 115, 123, 128, 131, 135
Mill, John Stuart, 13, 15
mind *(manas)*, 8, 13, 27, 51, 52, 59, 78–81, 99, 105, 107, 115, 136, 141
mindfulness *(satipaṭṭhāna)*, 52, 68, 77, 80–83
monarchism, 124
monarchy, 15, 124, 125, 127
monastic, 21, 131

Nāgārjuna, 106
necessity, 15, 35, 45; *(avitathatā)*, 94
net of Brahma, 70, 145
non-dual, 40, 54, 84
non-violence *(ahiṃsā)*, 23, 24, 59, 137, 138

objective pull, 3, 37
obligation, 4, 46, 60, 113
obsession *(papañca)*, 40, 42, 86, 121
omniscience *(sarvajñatā)*, 22, 27, 78, 82, 94, 95, 101

Pakudha Kaccāyana, 19
passion *(rāga)*, 31, 86, 90, 131
peace *(santi)*, 26, 77, 80–82, 116, 117; peaceful, 26, 27, 29, 35, 92, 123
Peirce, Charles Sanders, 39
perception *(saññā)*, 50, 51, 92, 104; cessation of, 30; content of, 31; process of, 40–43; unprejudiced, 81
permanence, 27, 29–32, 45, 46, 53, 86, 90, 92, 94, 96, 126
pessimism, 48
Plato, 37
Platonic, 34, 39, 60
Popper, Karl, 53
possibilities, 21, 32, 95
pragmatic, 16, 38, 39, 43–45, 143; pragmatism, 16, 39, 43
pre-determination, 19, 20
prohibition, 130, 131
psychology, 8, 21, 39, 40, 43, 48, 49, 90
psychophysical personality *(nāma-rūpa)*, 5, 8, 59, 61, 104, 105
punishment *(daṇḍa)*, 14, 24, 73, 98, 121, 127, 128, 133, 134
Pūraṇa Kassapa, 18, 19, 106
purity *(suddhi)*, 15, 19, 20, 67, 136, 139

radical empiricism, 31, 33, 39, 78, 113, 143
rationalism, 32, 39
rationality, 74, 135, 136, 139
Rawls, John, 135
reasoning, 23, 29, 32, 33, 40

rebirth, rebecoming *(punabbhava)*, 53, 60, 79, 88, 99, 103–106, 108, 144, 145
reflection, 43, 79, 81, 90, 131
renunciation, 9, 11, 26, 42, 44, 68, 78, 79, 87, 90, 127, 140
republicanism, 124, 125
restraint *(saṃvara)*, 15, 18, 86; absolute, 11; of emotions, 14; self-, 8; of the senses, 30, 68
retrocognition *(pubbenivāsānussati)*, 35, 103, 106
Russell, Bertrand, 38
revenge, 128, 133

sacred, 6, 9, 25
salt simile, 83, 85, 102
Sañjaya Bellaṭṭhiputta, 32
Sāṅkhya, 8, 9, 13
Sāriputta, 97
Schopenhauer, Arthur, 47, 48, 50
Schumacher, E. F., 119
secular, 25, 132
self *(ātma, atta)*, 4, 16, 20, 21, 32, 37, 45, 47, 48, 54, 56, 59, 92, 93, 100; -analysis, 131; -causation, 67; -control, 18; -deprivation, 59; desirous of, 60; -destructive, 85; empirical, 42; eternal, 8, 31, 50, 51, 59, 101, 104; harm of, 136; -indulgence, 59, 78, 86, 128, 131; -interest, 61, 114, 115, 119, 135; lump of dispositions, 51; -mortification, 78, 131; -nature, 19, 20; no-, 103; one-, 73, 100, 135, 136; -reliant, 89; -sacrifice, 9, 12, 60, 86, 119, 137; two selves, 5
skeptic, 32, 108
skepticism, 95
species, 19, 20, 74
specious present, 31–32
stages of life *(āśramadharma)*, 10–12, 14, 15, 21, 120
substance *(svabhāva)*, 8, 9, 30, 31, 50, 54, 68
substantialism, 30, 33, 92, 95
survival, 20, 25, 103, 104, 106–108

telepathy *(cetopariyañāṇa)*, 35
Theravāda, 84, 87
truth(s) *(satya, sacca, bhūta)*, 10, 27, 33, 43, 54, 73, 74, 127; absolutist and essentialist, 44; ineffability of, 34; of logic and mathematics, 38; noble *(ariya)*, 46, 79, 82; of science and logic, 35; terms for, 33; tripartite division of, 37; ultimate, 7, 8; and usefulness, 134

uniformity, 4, 83, 95, 145
Universal Monarch *(cakkavatti-rājā)*, 53, 120, 123, 125–127, 130, 131
universals, 55, 56
universe, 4, 36, 99
Upaniṣads (Upaniṣadic), 4, 6, 7, 9–11, 47, 48, 54, 55, 58, 59, 65, 84, 97
utilitarianism (utilitarian), 7, 10, 12, 13–16, 39, 119, 124, 135, 137

wager, 106–108
wealth, 13, 14, 58, 120, 122; enjoyment of, 11; generative of desire, 123; maldistribution of, 121; material, 121

DAVID J. KALUPAHANA is professor of philosophy at the University of Hawai'i. He has taught at the University of Sri Lanka (formerly University of Ceylon) and has studied as a British Council Research Scholar at the University of London, where he received his Ph.D. degree. He is the author of *A History of Buddhist Philosophy: Continuities and Discontinuities* (1992).

Production Notes

Composition and paging were done in
FrameMaker software on an AGFA AccuSet
Postscript Imagesetter by the design
and production staff of University of
Hawai'i Press.

The text typeface is Caledonia
and the display
typeface is Optima.

Offset presswork and binding were done by
The Maple-Vail Book Manufacturing Group.
Text paper is Glatfelter Smooth Antique, basis 50.